Roger Sherwood

Modern Housing Prototypes

Seventh printing, 2001

Publication of this book has been aided by a grant from
the Andrew W. Mellon Foundation.

Library of Congress Cataloging in Publication Data
Sherwood, Roger.
  Modern housing prototypes.

  Bibliography: p.
  1. Architecture, Domestic—Designs and plans. 2. Architecture, Modern —20th century—Designs and plans. I. Title.
NA7126.S48   728.3'1'0222   78-15508
ISBN 0-674-57941-0 (cloth)
ISBN 0-674-57942-9 (paper)

FOR DIANE

Acknowledgments

My work on this book would not have been possible without the generous support of the National Endowment for the Arts. I am grateful to the dedicated and enlightened staff of the Endowment, particularly William Lacey, former director of the Office of Architectural and Environmental Arts, for moral as well as financial support.

My colleagues and students at Cornell University and the University of Southern California have provided stimulus and encouragement. I owe a particular debt to Jim Tice, who helped with much of the drawing and was a sounding board for every idea. Special thanks are due to Larry Borins and Kalle Tavela, who assisted with the drawings; to Grover Gilchrist, who helped with the photographs; and to Alson Clark, head librarian of the School of Architecture and the Fine Arts Library at the University of Southern California, who tolerantly overlooked my occasional neglect of proper library procedures.

Finally, it was the people at Harvard University Press who brought this book to life. If *Modern Housing Prototypes* makes a useful contribution, it will be as much a result of their efforts as my own.

Grateful acknowledgment is made for permission to reproduce the following photographs and drawings. Illustrations in the Introduction are indicated by boldface figure numbers. Other illustrations are referred to by page number.

Karl Krämer Verlag: **3, 20, 25, 28** (Shadrach Woods, *Candilis-Josic-Woods*); 132b (Oscar Newman, *New Frontiers in Architecture*)

Verlagsanstalt Alexander Koch: **6, 72, 76, 77** (*Architektur und Wohnform*, February 1969); **16** (*Architektur und Wohnform*, May 1966); **64** (*Architektur und Wohnform*, January 1967)

Verlag Gerd Hatje: 10, 11, 34, 57 (K. W. Schmitt, *Multistory Housing*); 26, 27, 35, 66 (Wolfgang Pehnt, *German Architecture, 1960–1970*); 42, 54 (Hubert Hoffmann, *Row Houses and Cluster Houses*); 55 (Klaus Franck, *The Works of Affonso Eduardo Reidy*); 132c (Robert Maxwell, *New British Architecture*)

Artemis Verlag: **12, 46, 82,** 83a, 83b, 85a, 85c, 97c, 98a, 98b, 115a, 115b, 120a, 120b, 125a, 130c, 132a (Le Corbusier, *Oeuvre complète*); **14, 33,** 108a, 108b, 111a, 111b, 111c, 149a, 149c, 151a, 151b, 154b, 157a (Karl Fleig, ed., *Alvar Aalto, 1963–1970*); **43,** 162a (Knud Bastlund, *José Luis Sert*); **69** (Alfred Roth, *La Nouvelle Architecture*); 42a, 44a (Werner Blaser, *Mies van der Rohe*)

Architectural Design: **13, 45, 47, 58, 61, 66b, 71a** (September 1967); **48,** 62a, 62b, 65a (February 1963); **53** (November 1964); **60** (December 1961); **63** (July 1968); **81** (January 1964)

R. M. Schindler Architecture Collection, University Art Galleries, University of California, Santa Barbara: **15,** 31a, 33a, 34a, 34b, 34c, 34d, 35a, 35b, 36a

The Frank Lloyd Wright Foundation: **17,** 29a, 30a (first copyrighted 1948 by

Contents

Block Housing

Slabs

Towers

Modern Housing Prototypes

Introduction

This book is presented in the belief that a reexamination of some of the great housing projects of this century is appropriate at a time when the design of housing commands the attention of architects the world around. The buildings offered here as case studies were selected because of their importance as prototypes, projects that set the standards and patterns of much that was, and is, to follow. Other considerations were diversity—so that a wide range of countries, building types, and problems would be represented—and architectural quality. My assumption is that there is no excuse for poor architecture; that housing, like all buildings, to paraphrase Geoffrey Scott, must be convenient to use, soundly built, *and* beautiful.

But why prototypes? One of the essential points of heuristic thought—the process of discovery and invention relating to problem solving—is the awareness that, until a problem is clearly defined, guesses or conjectures must be made to help clarify the problem. During the period of uncertainty, reference to analogous problems can be used to give a new turn to one's thinking. Through the study of solutions to related problems, a fresh conclusion may be reached.

Various writers have suggested that it is never possible to state all the dimensions of a problem, that "truly quantifiable criteria always leave choices for the designer to make."[1] In the absence of clear design determinants, and to avoid purely intuitive guessing, it has been argued that analogous reference might give design insight; that perhaps a paradigm of the problem might be accepted as a provisional solution, or an attack on the problem might be made by adapting the solution to a previous problem; that during the period when many of the variables are unknown, a "typology of forms" might be used as a simulative technique to clarify the problem.

The notion of using an analogous problem as a paradigm for gaining insight into a present problem is not, of course, new. A mathematician typically looks for an auxiliary theorem having the same or a similar conclusion.[2] In architec-

1. Alan Colquhoun, "Typology and Design Method," *Arena*, 1967, pp. 11–14. Karl Popper has perhaps best articulated the notion that logical heuristic process can be stimulated in situations characterized by a lack of quantifiable data by offering tentative solutions and then criticizing these solutions. Popper's book *Conjectures and Refutations* (New York: Basic Books, 1962) is a lengthy justification of this procedure. William Bartley, "How Is the House of Science Built," *Architectural Association Journal,* February 1965, pp. 213–218, summarizes Popper's thesis as follows: "The first job of the man who has a problem must be to become better acquainted with it. The way to do this is by producing an inadequate solution to the problem—a speculation—and by criticizing this. To understand a problem means, in effect, to understand its difficulties; and this cannot be done until we see why the more obvious solutions do not work. Even in those cases where no satisfactory answer turns up we may learn something from this procedure" (p. 216). Max Black also deals with the idea of analogous reference or model in *Models and Metaphors* (Ithaca: Cornell University Press, 1962), especially chapter 13, "Models and Archetypes."

2. See G. Polya, *How to Solve It* (New York: Doubleday, 1957).

1
Harumi Apartment House, Tokyo. Kunio Maekawa, 1958.
2
Park Hill, Sheffield. Lewis Womersley, 1959.
3
Housing, Morocco. ATBAT, 1950.

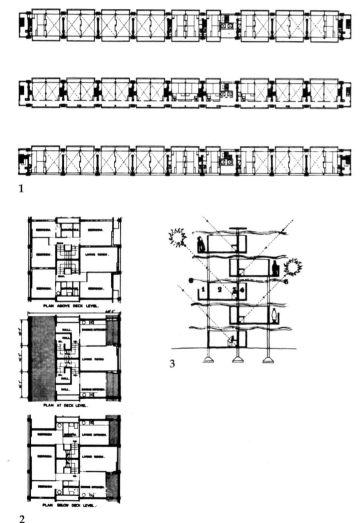

1

2

ture, invention often passes through a phase of groping, where ideas about a projected building form are triggered by exposure to some existing building with a similar program, functional specification, or site condition. The analogous building then becomes in some sense a model or a prototype.

The use of prototypes is especially useful in the design of housing because housing lends itself readily to systematic, typological study. Most building types, such as theaters, schools, factories, or even office buildings, have to respond to different programs and are rarely consistent and repetitive. Housing, because it consists of repeating units with a constant relation to vertical and horizontal circulation, can more logically be studied in terms of its typological variations. Although housing would seem to embrace almost unlimited possible variations, in fact there are not many basic organizational possibilities and each housing type can be categorized fairly easily.

While building regulations, construction techniques, and housing needs have considerable impact on the form that housing may take at any given time in any given culture, still only a few dwelling unit types are plausible, and these units may be collected together in only a few rather limited ways that do not change very much from country to country. An apartment building today in Zagreb—as an organization of living units—is much like an apartment building in Berlin or Tokyo. Even extreme cultural requirements, such as the provisions for a tatami life-style in Maekawa's Harumi slab in Tokyo of 1958 (1), have resulted in an organization that can easily be compared to a Western model; Park Hill in Sheffield of the sixties (2), for example, is organizationally similar. Both have larger and smaller units in the typical section. Entrance to the larger of the two—a two-level unit—is at the corridor level, with rooms above; stairs lead to the smaller unit below. In each, therefore, the corridor occurs at every other level, and stairs lead up and down from there. Although the position of the stairs, kitchen, and bath are different—along parallel walls in Harumi and in a zone parallel to the corridor in Park Hill—and the sitings of the buildings are quite different, nevertheless they are organized fundamentally alike. Even the Arab housing designed in Morocco in the fifties by ATBAT (3), where cultural requirements dictated absolute visual privacy, outdoor cooking, and a lack of the usual room subdivisions and conventional toilets, resulted in a building which, although it has a peculiar checkerboard elevation, is more or less a conventional single-loaded, gallery-access apartment building.

Whatever his cultural, economic, and technical constraints, every architect is confronted with choices and questions about organization. How will the individual apartment be arranged? How will the mix of different apartment types be accommodated? What circulation systems—horizontal and vertical—can service this mix of apartments? What is the best circulation system? Walk-up or single-loaded, double-loaded, or skip-stop corridor system? Where is entrance and access to the vertical circulation system? What building form does this collection of units take: low-rise or high-rise, rowhouse, slab, or tower? These fundamental organizational questions are pertinent to any housing project. *Modern Housing Prototypes* is intended to provide the architect with a set of analogous references to help him solve these basic organizational problems.

Unit Types
Beginning with basic apartments or units, only two are suitable for repetitive use; one other—the 90° double-orientation unit—has limited application. The basic types are:

4
Sorgenfri apartment block, Malmö, Sweden. Jaenecke and Samuelson, 1959.

5
Lincoln Estate, London. Martin, Bennett, and Lewis, 1960.

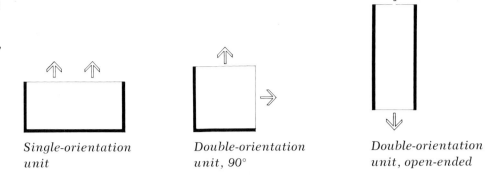

Single-orientation unit

Double-orientation unit, 90°

Double-orientation unit, open-ended

Each of these three unit types has several typical variations, depending upon the positioning of core elements—kitchen, bath, and stairs (when used inside the unit)—the entrance options, and the depths necessary for natural light. Minimum unit dimensions vary from country to country as building regulations and construction practices differ, and the arrangement of core elements, natural light, and ventilation requirements change from place to place.

Single-Orientation Unit

Units that open or face to one side come in two types: with core elements arranged along transverse walls, perpendicular to the corridor, or arranged in an interior zone adjacent and parallel to the corridor. Although these units have a preferred side—they face outward and are most often used where three sides are closed except for the entrance from the corridor (a typical double-loaded corridor arrangement)—some single-loaded, open gallery-access versions may have some minor windows opening to the gallery.

Single-orientation unit; transverse core. This type has the advantage of using the transverse structural wall for core elements, so that most plumbing and mechanical stacks are adjacent to structural walls in a back-to-back arrangement between units. The obvious disadvantage with the type is that the kitchen and in some cases the bath are taking up exterior surface which could be better used for living and sleeping areas, since under many building codes the kitchen and bath do not require natural light and ventilation. An awkward plan can result when the kitchen is on one transverse wall and the bath on the other. Also, the blank exterior walls that core elements tend to create (especially with the small windows typically used in a kitchen or bath) generate elevational problems; these blank surfaces also contradict the preferred-side characteristics of the type.

The typical unit may include a scheme where the kitchen and bath are together on one wall with the kitchen to the outside, like the Sorgenfri block in Malmö, Sweden, by Jaenecke and Samuelson (4). Other variations include two-story units such as the Lincoln Estate slab by J. L. Martin (5). Here two units interlock around an interior core of stairs and toilets; the kitchen in each unit is in a zone along the transverse wall on one side of the building. Park Hill (2) has a similar arrangement although it employs an alternate level corri-

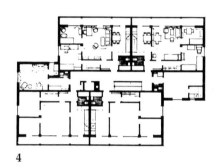

4

5

6
Apartments, Baltimore. Mies van der Rohe, c. 1965.
7
Lake Shore Drive apartments, Chicago. Mies van der Rohe, 1948.
8
Lamble Street housing, London. Powell and Moya, 1954.
9
Courtyard housing, Espoo, Finland. Korhonen and Laapotti, c. 1968.
10
Neue Vahr Apartments, Bremen. Alvar Aalto, 1958.
11
Preston housing, Lancashire. Stirling and Gowan, 1961.

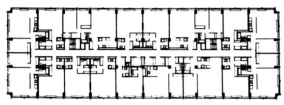

6

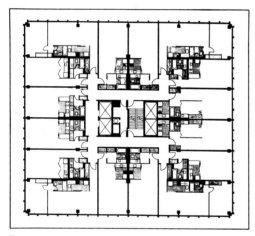

7

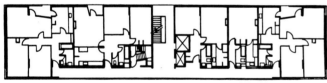

8

dor; the floors above and below the corridor level are double-orientation unit types (open both front and rear), with the kitchens lining up on one side of the building.

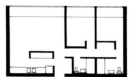

Single-orientation unit; interior core along the corridor. In the more common type of single-orientation unit, the core elements are arranged in a zone parallel and adjacent to the corridor. Entrance is through this zone into the main spaces of the apartment, thus letting the major rooms open to the preferred side of the building. The kitchen and bath are interior spaces with mechanical ventilation. This simpler plan usually features a compact back-to-back kitchen and bath grouping and clear, consistent zoning of spaces. The double-loaded corridor slabs designed by Mies van der Rohe (6) are planned this way. He modifies the idea slightly in the Lake Shore Drive apartments (7), where the bath and kitchen are back-to-back but the kitchen opens to the major spaces on the preferred side. Although more typically a plan for double-loaded corridor buildings (where apartments are located on both sides of the corridor), the type is also used for single-loaded or access-gallery plans. The Lamble Street project by Powell and Moya (8) is an example of this type. Or, for a lower density type, there are the courtyard houses by Korhonen and Laapotti in Finland (9).

Aalto's apartments at Bremen (10), an unusual variation of the single-orientation type, consist of fan-shaped units opening out to the site. Core elements here, although placed along transverse structural walls, are nevertheless in an interior zone along the corridor. The Preston housing by Stirling and Gowan (11) is a two-story version of the same type. These two are single-loaded corridor examples, but the single-orientation unit type is probably most advantageous where three sides of the unit are closed, implying a double-loaded, corridor-every-floor organization.

A common variation of the singly-oriented unit (applicable to units with either transverse or interior core) works from a strategy of increasing the exterior surface on the open side of the unit so that more rooms can get light and

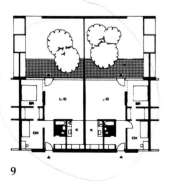

9

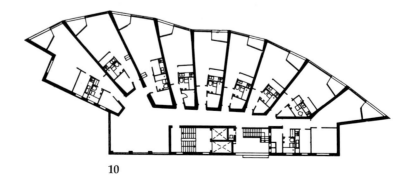

10

11

12
Immeuble Villas project. Le Corbusier, 1922.
13
Bishopsfield and Charters Cross, Harlow, Essex. Michael Neyland, 1960.
14
Hansaviertel apartments, Berlin. Alvar Aalto, 1956.
15
El Pueblo Ribera patio houses, La Jolla. R. M. Schindler, 1923.

air. Le Corbusier's Immeuble Villas projects of the twenties (12) were of this type: L-shaped units around an open terrace. Although the Immeuble Villas are two-story units with minor windows on the corridor side of the upper floor of each unit, implying a double orientation, the zoning of large volumes and terraces to one side contribute to a definite preferred condition. This type can work in a single- or double-loaded situation. Bishopsfield and Charters Cross housing at Harlow by Michael Neyland (13) is another example of a repeating L-plan, in this case, double-loaded with corridor walls containing only minor windows to the kitchens.

Aalto's Hansa apartments in Berlin (14) are basically a singly-oriented type that follows the strategy of increasing exterior surface: its U-plan features dining, living, and bedrooms all around a central terrace. Schindler's El Pueblo Ribera houses at La Jolla (15) are also single-orientation, U-shaped units coupled together in pairs with hedges used to define and enclose the courtyard spaces.

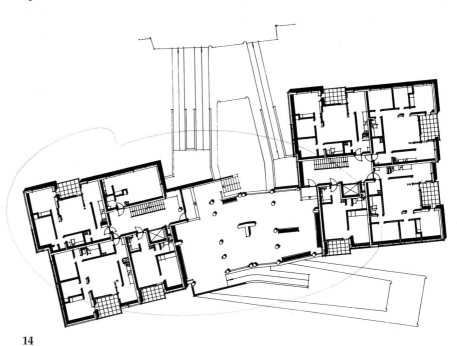

14

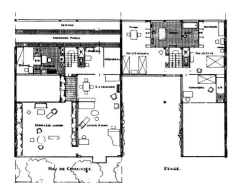

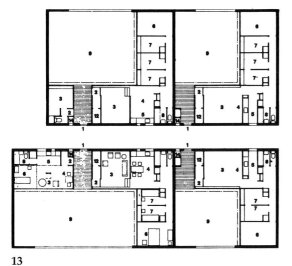

12

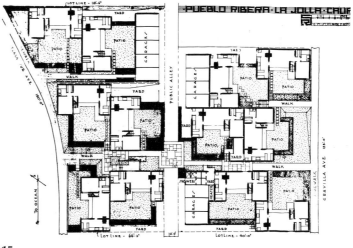

13

15

16
Patio housing, Frankfurt. Egon Eiermann, 1966.
17
Cloverleaf project. Frank Lloyd Wright, 1939.
18
St. Mark's Tower, project. Wright, 1929.
19
Atrium houses, Schwerzenback, Switzerland. Fred Kunz, 1967.

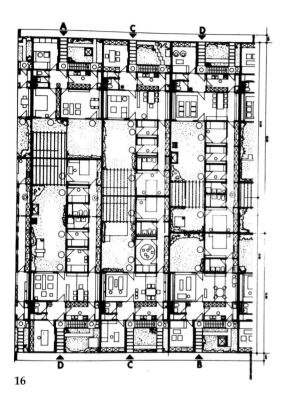

16

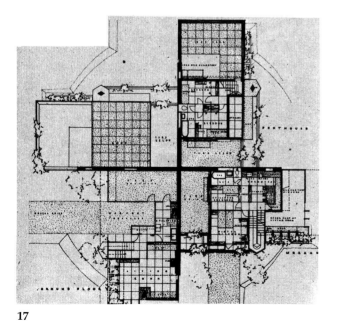

17

A possible variation of the single-orientation type is the matte housing scheme, where a matrix of walls is built with each unit inside a walled-in area. Access requirements limit the number of collective arrangements possible, but Egon Eiermann's matte housing in Frankfurt of 1966 (16) is an example of this type. Although there are small private gardens on the entrance side of each apartment, most major spaces open to a private garden to the rear, establishing the single orientation.

Double-Orientation Unit, 90°

Double-orientation unit types come in many variations and can be collected together in many different ways. The corner type or 90° double-orientation unit may be seen simply as a singly-oriented unit in which one of the three closed walls has been opened up. This limits the strategies of collecting units together, since each needs a corner, and the use of this type seems to be limited to towers, smaller freestanding buildings, and to certain kinds of terrace housing.

Frank Lloyd Wright's Suntop Homes are a good example of this type: four units within crossed party walls, each three stories high opening at the corner. Wright's earlier versions like the Cloverleaf development (17) introduced an internal courtyard. St. Mark's Tower (18) and the built version of it, the Bartlesville Price Tower, adopt the same parti of four corner units with core elements on the interior. Buildings employing this kind of unit necessarily must be freestanding, with private entrance required for projects like Suntop and common lobbies for towers like Bartlesville.

Other examples of one- or two-story corner units include the atrium houses at Schwerzenback in Switzerland by Kunz (19) and the Candilis, Josic, and Woods projects, which often consist of buildings planned to gain the corner advantage even to the extent of creating site arrangements consisting of many staggered-plan buildings in an overall system designed to maximize peripheral

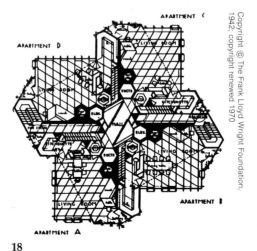

18

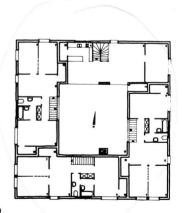

19

20
Cluster housing project. Candilis, Josic, and Woods, 1959.
21
Tower, Vallingby, Sweden. Ancker and Gate, 1953.
22
Nirwana Apartments, Den Haag. Johannes Duiker, 1927.
23
Hansaviertel tower, Berlin. Luciano Baldessari, 1956.
24
The Albany Houses, New York. Fellheimer, Wagner, and Vollmer, 1950.

surface (20). Most compact towers use this type: for example, the Vallingby tower by Ancker and Gate (21) or the Nirwana apartment buildings by Duiker (22), which have a much larger area in plan but are organized with an apartment in each corner.

Various permutations of the tower use a strategy of creating more exterior surface and hence more corner conditions. While many of these are not strictly 90° units, they are versions of the corner unit in that they cannot be repeated in linear fashion like the singly-oriented types. The Baldessari tower in the Hansa project in Berlin (23) or the Albany Houses in Brooklyn by Fellheimer, Wagner, and Vollmer, done for the New York City Housing Authority (24), are examples of this variation. Pinwheel plans such as the Candilis, Josic, and

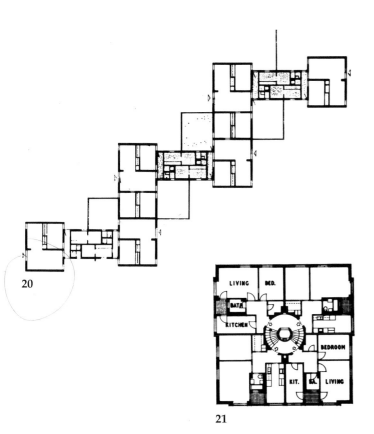

20

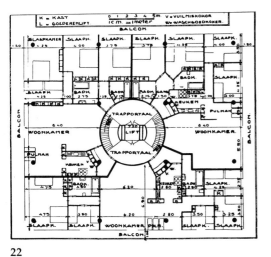

21

22

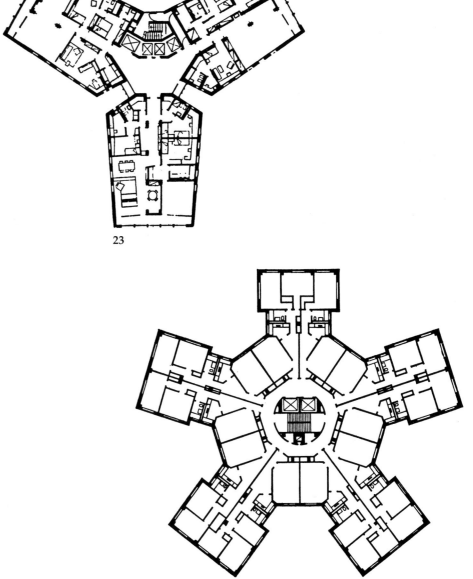

23

24

25
Apartment block, Bagnols sur Ceze, France. Candilis, Josic, and Woods, 1957.
26
Märkischesviertel, Berlin, floor plan. O. M. Ungers, 1962.
27
Märkischesviertel, Berlin, site plan. O. M. Ungers, 1962.
28
Housing block, Clos d'Orville, Nîmes. Candilis, Josic, and Woods, 1961.
29
Tower, Copenhagen. A/S Dominia, c. 1960.

Woods project at Bagnols sur Ceze of 1957 (25) try to maximize the corner situation. O. M. Ungers employed this idea with a slightly different variation in the Märkischesviertel project in Berlin in 1962 (26). Here bedrooms are put into the corners, which are solid except for small windows; the leftover void is designated as living space. Essentially, it is a corner, pinwheel parti that generates—when used in combination—a distinctive staggered site plan (27). This was a popular idea at Märkischesviertel, and many architects besides Ungers used it. All these projects are perhaps derived from various Candilis, Josic, and Woods schemes for cluster housing in the mid-fifties, where pinwheel blocks or towers hook up with each other to make a kind of continuous building (28).

Still other strategies to increase peripheral surface and mulitply corners are the slipped-slab schemes such as this by A/S Dominia in Copenhagen (29).

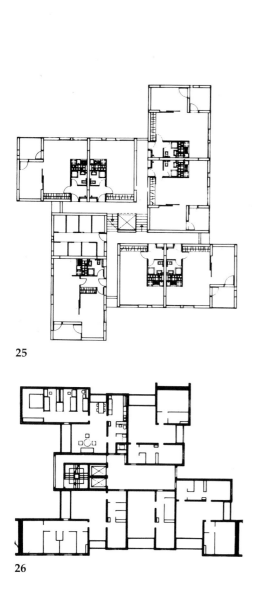

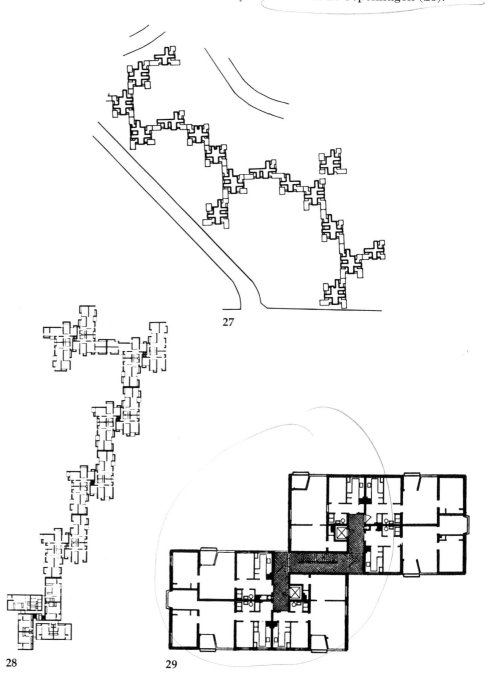

25

26

27

28

29

30
Bethnal Green towers, London. Denys Lasdun, 1960.

31
Zollikerberg terrace housing, Zurich. Marti and Kast, 1964.

32
Terrace housing, Zug, Switzerland. Stucky and Meuli, c. 1960.

33
Terrace housing, Kauttua, Finland. Alvar Aalto, 1938.

34
Apartment tower, St. James Place, London. Denys Lasdun, 1960.

Lasdun in the Bethnal Green towers (30) uses the same idea, as does Aalto with the Hansa block in Berlin (14).

Some terrace housing projects utilize a more complex version of the 90° or corner unit. The Zollikerberg project in Zurich by Marti and Kast (31) is an example of this. Here two-story L-shaped atrium units are placed on top of one another and stepped up a slope, with a retaining wall against the slope. Side walls are punctured only with small windows. There is a preferred condition toward the garden, but the living room becomes the dominant void at one corner. The Stucky and Meuli units also in Switzerland (32) step up a slope, again with the windowless retaining wall against the slope and with essentially closed walls on the two sides. All major rooms open to a continuous terrace, and the living room, which is the main space, opens to two sides at the corner. The above examples are not, strictly speaking, just 90° units because each apartment has openings to three sides and does not attach horizontally to other units; however, the positioning of the living room as a large volume at the corner emphasizes the corner condition. The drawing of the Aalto terrace houses at Kauttua (33) shows this condition three-dimensionally with openings to three sides. But this is only suitable on very narrow sites, and a more typical condition perhaps would be side-by-side Kauttuas with each unit more literally a corner type. Denys Lasdun's beautiful apartment block at St. James Place in London of 1960 (34) is a high-rise example of the same condition. Although it is a tower backed up to an existing party wall on one side with open space on the other three sides, it is spatially a 90° type. By use of an ingenious split-level section, Lasdun has been able to further accentuate the corner orientation of the living room, which is one and one-half floors high and opens to a park on the preferred side of the building.

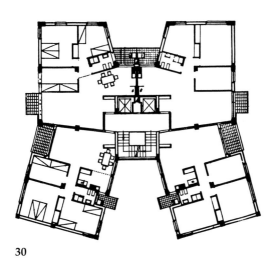

30

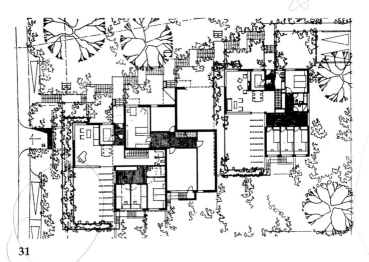

31

32

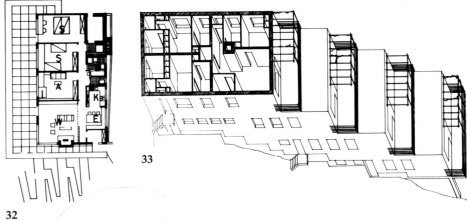

33

34

35
Green Belt South housing, Zollstock, Germany. O. M. Ungers, 1965.
36
Patio housing, Tustin, California. Backen, Arrigoni, and Ross, 1969.
37
Rowhouses, Werkbund Exhibition, Vienna. André Lurçat, 1932.
38
Siemensstadt housing, Berlin. Fred Forbat, 1930.

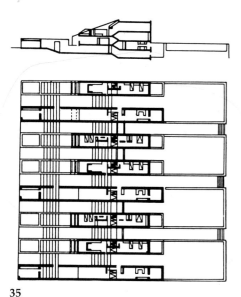

35

36

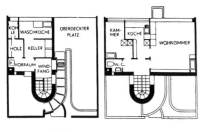

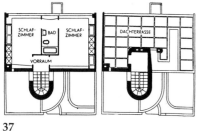

37

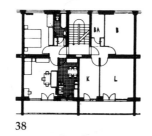

38

Double-Orientation Unit, Open-Ended

While single-orientation units are suitable for buildings with double-loaded corridors that open to each side and for hillside housing or single-loaded corridor buildings that turn their backs upon some undesirable site condition such as a highway or a northern exposure, housing units with a double orientation are far more common. Probably stemming from the common sense advantage of repeating units while still maintaining maximum exterior surface, this system of placing open-ended units side by side is perhaps the oldest form of collective urban housing. A dwelling unit that is open at each end has many organizational options. If the unit is very deep, light is minimal and the open ends are not much of an advantage. O. M. Ungers' Green Belt South housing of 1965 (35) or the Backen, Arrigoni, and Ross project in Tustin (36) are good examples of very deep units. In each, the unit is so long that some auxiliary means of lighting the interior has been used. With Ungers, a parallel open slot lets light into the four-story building, while in the Tustin project a system of interior courtyards is used, resulting in a one-story building.

By comparison, units such as Lurçat's rowhouses at the Vienna Werkbund Exposition (37) do not have a light problem because they are so shallow. But because the rooms are small, core elements come to an outside wall and the stairs are actually attached to the exterior as a separate element. So there are general criteria for optimum depth: shallower units could very well become single-orientation types, deeper units have to find some other means of introducing light, such as interior courtyards (which are unsuitable for high-rise buildings). Optimum widths and depths are also a function of building requirements: room sizes, stairs, and so on.

The open-ended slot requires open space outside the unit at each end and usually some means of providing privacy—a garden wall, for example—except where the unit is well off the ground. Access to this type can be from either end or, in the case of multistory buildings, from within, making internal skip-stop corridor systems mandatory. Walk-up units, which were especially popular in Europe before the postwar proliferation of high-rise building—Siemensstadt, for example (38)—also give access at an interior point.

Generally, the double-orientation type is at least a two-story unit, so the architect must consider where the stair, kitchen, and bath can be put. Basically, the types may be classified as either transverse (stair perpendicular to the long axis of the unit) or longitudinal (stair parallel to the long axis). Following are a few examples of the double-orientation types.

39
Procuratie Nuove, Venice. Vincenzo Scamozzi, seventeenth century.
40
Typical townhouse, Baltimore. Nineteenth century.
41
Rowhouses, Reston, Virginia. Whittlesey and Conklin, 1964.
42
Rowhouses, Roehampton. London County Council, 1952.

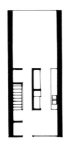

Double-orientation unit, open-ended; interior stair and core, longitudinal stair. Sometimes called a "dumbbell" plan because of its form—a void at each end and a concentration of parts in the middle—this type positions the major living spaces to the outside, where an opening to private outdoor space is a possibility, and keeps the core elements, including the stairs, on the interior. The dumbbell plan rowhouse has a tradition dating back to medieval times and in most Western cities was probably the most common form of housing until the invention of the rigid structural frame. Historic examples are wide-ranging: Scamozzi's Procuratie Nuove of the seventeenth century in Venice (39) is entered from an interior courtyard via stairs, with major living spaces facing the Piazza San Marco and sleeping spaces opening to the garden and the Grand Canal—palatial quarters ingeniously planned, of incredible beauty. On the other hand one may find a rowhouse from Baltimore of the nineteenth century, which is typical of urban housing in the eastern part of the United States prior to 1920 or so (40). The dumbbell plan is popular in the United States because building codes allow interior kitchens and baths. Other examples include the rowhouses at Reston (41) and those at Roehampton by the London County Council (42).

The typical early twentieth-century walk-up housing consisted of a dumbbell plan that was entered from an interior hallway. Even though European building codes tend to require that kitchens have exterior windows, a dumbbell type

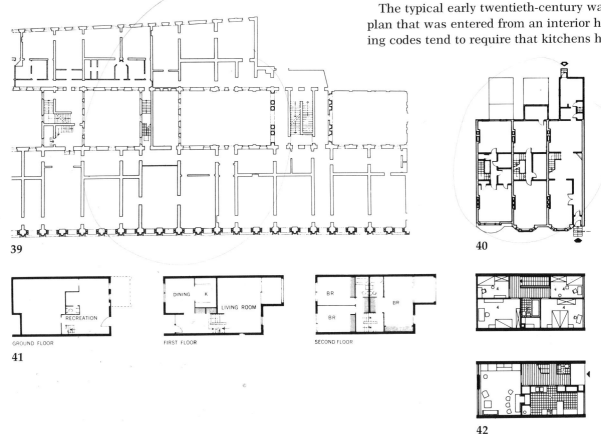

39

40

41   GROUND FLOOR   FIRST FLOOR   SECOND FLOOR   DINING   K   LIVING ROOM   RECREATION   BR   BR   BR

42

43
Peabody Terrace, Cambridge, Massachusetts. Sert, Jackson, and Gourley, 1964.
44
Weissenhof exhibition housing, Stuttgart. Mies van der Rohe, 1927.
45
King Street housing, London. Morton, Lupton, and Smith, 1967.
46
Unité d'Habitation, Marseilles. Le Corbusier, 1952.

of plan usually results. Examples are Sert's Peabody Terrace at Harvard (43) and Siemensstadt (38), the huge project outside Berlin of the 1930s. There one finds many different buildings done by many different architects, but all are just minor variations of the same unit type—a situation probably encouraged, in Germany at least, by Mies van der Rohe's block at the Stuttgart Weissenhof exhibition of 1927 (44). This is the type of walk-up unit that was used in Germany to the practical exclusion of all else for almost two decades. The walk-up unit with a dumbbell plan is also popular in England, the King Street project by Morton, Lupton, and Smith (45) perhaps being representative of recent rowhousing there.

The dumbbell plan is not restricted to use in rowhouses or walk-up situations. It also has wide application in high-rise buildings, particularly slabs. Le Corbusier's Unité d'Habitation (46), a building that has been repeated in

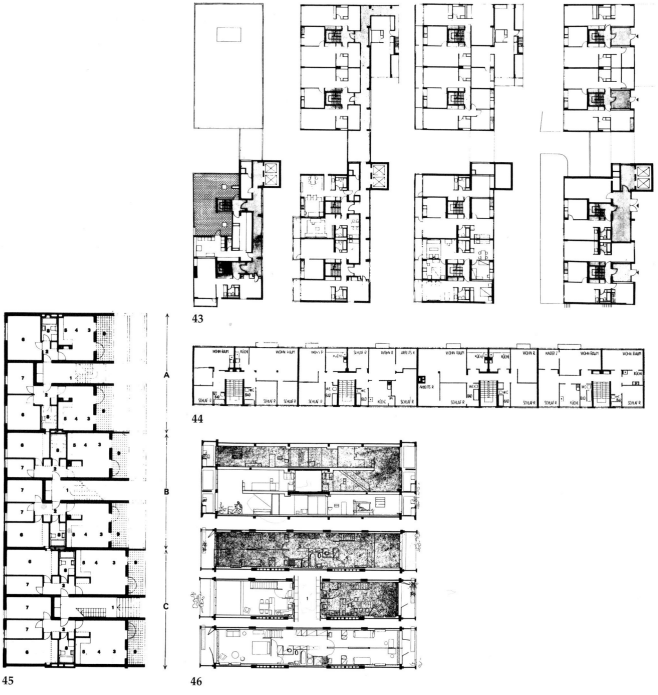

43

44

45

46

47
Milton Road rowhouses, London. District of Haringey, 1967.
48
Siedlung Halen, Bern. Atelier 5, 1959.

slightly differing versions in France and Germany and has been widely copied almost everywhere, is the perfect example of a multistory dumbbell plan. A double-loaded, skip-stop corridor gives access to a two-level unit with kitchen, dining, and living area at entry level and bedrooms and bath above. Here the core elements, including the stair, are interior, although the stair rises from a double-height living room.

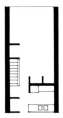

Double-orientation unit, open-ended; exterior kitchen, longitudinal stair. Perhaps a more common version of the longitudinal stair arrangement, and one popular in Europe, brings the kitchen to the outside; either the bath for the bedrooms is above the kitchen or another core or service wall is introduced on the interior. Examples of this include the Milton Road project (47) and Siedlung Halen by Atelier 5 (48), both self-contained rowhouses or terrace houses, or a walk-up situation also from the Milton Road project by the Borough of Haringey (47). This unit type is also used in high-rise slabs but again, because it is a two-story unit, it is limited to skip-stop corridor arrangements. Single-

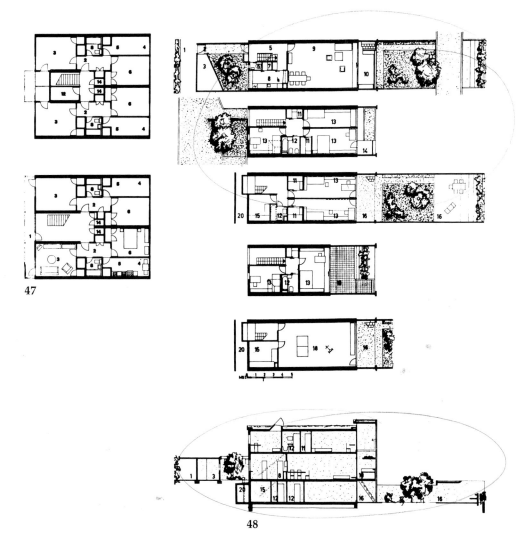

47

48

49
Apartments, Germany. Schmiedel and Zumpe, 1960.
50
Hansaviertel tower, Berlin. Van den Broek and Bakema, 1956.
51
L'Aero Habitat, Algiers. Bourlier and Ferrier, 1950.
52
Hillside housing, Ithaca, New York. Werner Seligmann, 1972.
53
Swiss Cottage, London. Douglas Stephen, 1960.

loaded and double-loaded corridor arrangements are feasible, with the kitchen usually at the entrance level; in the case of the single-loaded type with access gallery, the kitchen gets light from the gallery. Examples of the double-loaded type include Schmiedel's apartments in Germany (49) and the van den Broek and Bakema Hansa block in Berlin (50).

Single-loaded versions include the L'Aero Habitat development by Bourlier and Ferrier in Algiers of 1950 (51), Werner Seligmann's hillside housing in Ithaca, New York, of 1972 (52), and Swiss Cottage in London by Douglas Stephen with Koulermos and Forrest (53).

Double-orientation unit, open-ended; exterior kitchen, transverse stair. This is the most common open-ended unit. Although usually wider than a unit with a longitudinal stair, several advantages result. First, a clear circulation zone along one wall is defined by the stairs and other core functions along the opposite wall. Circulation in the living room is now along the side of the space, and from the entrance one can see down the hallway into the living area, which gives the impression of one continuous space throughout the floor. If the stair is pulled back slightly from each side wall, allowing enough space to move past the stair, the kitchen can serve the living and dining area past the stair without using the main hallway. This unit satisfies the European preference for exterior-fronting kitchens and forms a larger space in the living and dining area where it is most useful. Upstairs, unless the plumbing stack can be manipulated so that the bathroom is on the interior, valuable exterior surface is taken up with a space requiring only minimal light and air. Either single-run or return stairs can be used, and different minimum unit widths, of course, re-

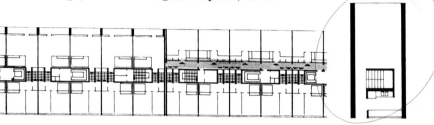

49

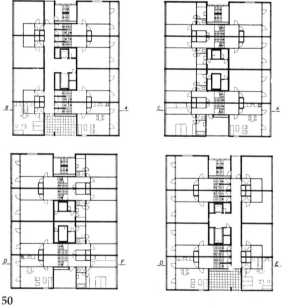

50

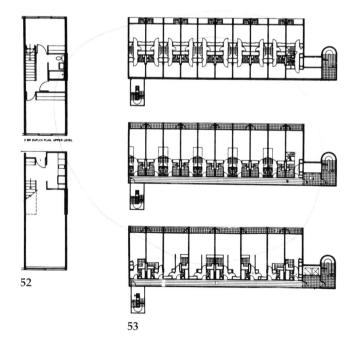

52

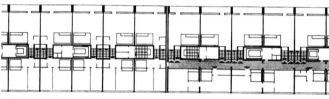

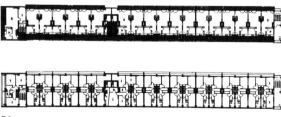

51

53

14

54
Flamatt terrace housing, Bern. Atelier 5, 1960.
55
Pedregulho housing, Rio de Janeiro. Affonso Reidy, 1950.
56
Unité Billardon, Dijon. Pierre Beck, 1954.
57
Terrace apartments, Germany. Schroder and Frey, 1959.

sult. Low-rise examples include the Flamatt terrace houses in Bern by Atelier 5 (54) and their famous Siedlung Halen, also in Bern (48).

This is a common type for use in high-rise buildings. The serpentine slab of Affonso Reidy in the Pedregulho development in Rio de Janeiro (55), the Billardon slab at Dijon by Beck (56), and Womersley's Park Hill project (2) are three examples.

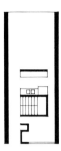

Double-orientation unit, open-ended; interior kitchen, transverse stair. This version of the dumbbell type, with stair and other core elements on the interior, comes in many variations, some with stair, kitchen, and bath on the same side, some with the kitchen opposite the stair. Examples of the latter arrangement include the terraced walk-up flats of Schroder and Frey (57). Sometimes

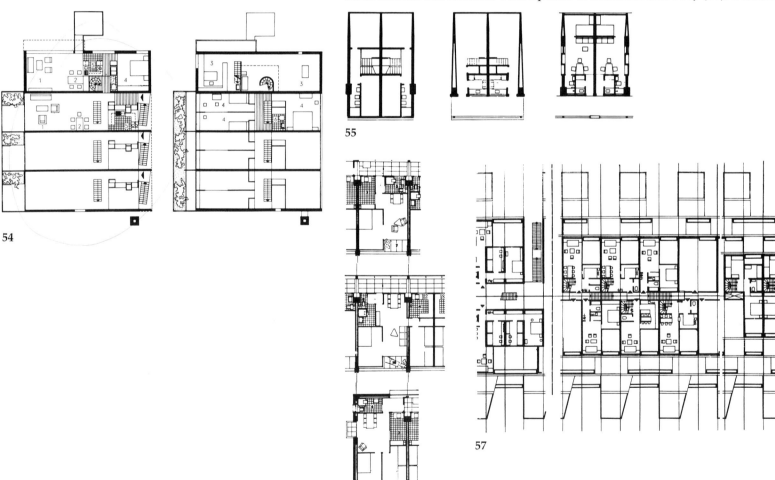

54

55

56

57

15

58
Edith Avenue housing, Durham, England. Napper, Errington, Collerton, Barnett, and Allot, 1961.
59
Rowhouses, Hampstead. Amis and Howell, 1956.
60
Quinta Normal, Santiago. Carlos Bresciani, 1960.
61
Fleet Road terrace housing, London. Neave Brown, 1968.
62
Apartment block, Lausanne. Decoppet, Veuve, Aubry, and Miéville, 1959.

the transverse stair and the kitchen are together, a type common in row-house applications—for example, the Edith Avenue housing project of 1961 in Durham (58), and the Amis and Howell houses in Hampstead of 1956 (59).

Few high-rise buildings seem to use this type. However, the Bresciani project, Quinta Normal in Santiago, Chile (60), uses an interlocking system with living and dining areas and kitchen taking up two bays to one side of the corridor at the lower floor and the bedrooms in an open-ended arrangement above but in just one bay. This system would be applicable for high-rise slabs as well.

The double-orientation, dumbbell unit plan is impractical for very shallow buildings where there is seldom room for the interior core. In Lurcat's Vienna project (37), for example, the core has to come to the outside, although here each unit is three floors high. With Neave Brown's Fleet Road project (61), a similar situation occurs: a three-bedroom maisonette has kitchen and bath fronting the gallery, but, because of the limited area on any one floor, a peculiar mix of spaces results in which the dining area is separated from the living room, bedrooms are on both floors, and toilet facilities are of necessity duplicated. For high-rise building, this type is probably not suitable: a very narrow building would be structurally unstable if higher than a few floors unless the building were warped for added lateral support. The Smithsons' curved slab project of the 1950s (page 132) was presumably developed just for this reason.

Another double-orientation, open-ended unit type that is widely used expands laterally; bedrooms, rather than being upstairs, take over the adjacent bay, so that the entire apartment is on one floor but in two bays. In a two-story unit, there is an overlapping of bays so that bedrooms above would be over the living rooms of both units below. The single-floor version is typical of most walk-up housing or noncorridor types of high-rise buildings. The Decoppet, Veuve, Aubry, and Mieville project in Lausanne, Switzerland (62), is a good example of this type.

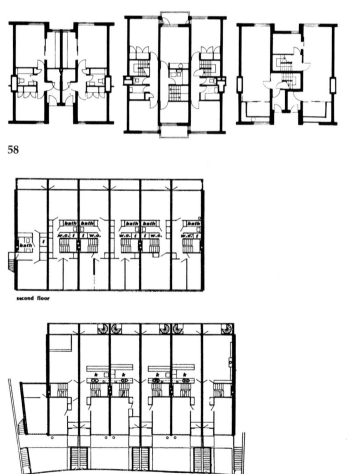

58

59

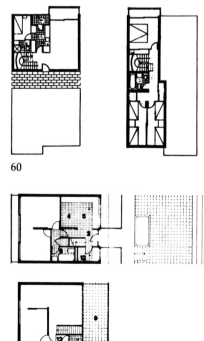

60

61

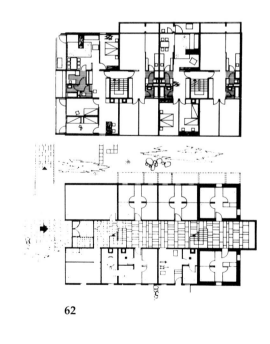

62

Winscombe Street houses, London. Neave Brown, 1968.

Building Types

The ways in which the various dwelling units can be combined into different building forms are a function of the special characteristics of the building—site, orientation, height, and so on—and the circulation system used. Because the ways in which units may be collected together are limited by building regulations, construction practices, and cultural preferences, different housing types occur in some countries while not in others. For example, United States fire codes, until very recently, required an exit from each floor of an apartment and so eliminated skip-stop sections like the typical Unité of Le Corbusier. In some countries, such as France and Brazil, multiple fire stairs are not required; and in Chile five-story walk-ups are allowed. Sometimes a particular housing form may result from a tradition of similar housing: the widespread construction of four-story walk-up buildings in Germany, the gallery-access maisonette in England, or hillside housing in Switzerland. Although absolute comparison of housing from country to country would have to take into consideration the differences in building regulations, construction practices, and national traditions, comparison is possible on the basis of unit and building types. It is not necessary to understand all about building in a particular place to be able to analyze a particular building, to classify it organizationally, and to identify its unique features and concepts. Without a comprehensive understanding of building practices in every country—an unlikely knowledge—comparison on any other basis seems all but impossible.

Building forms resulting from the collecting together of many units into a single building are closely tied to a few possible circulation options. If a community of dwellings is seen as simply many individual houses, each hooking on to an access system, then only a few systems emerge.

Private Access

Here there is private entrance and private internal vertical circulation. Height is limited by most building codes to two or three stories. Units cannot be stacked vertically and the idea is restricted to rowhouses, detached houses, or terrace houses. Neave Brown's five houses on Winscombe Street in London (63) are examples of this type.

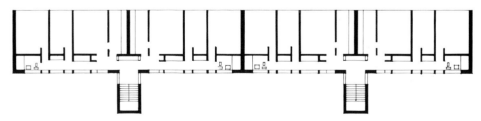

Multiple Vertical Access

This type can be built up to five stories without elevators in some countries, but more often three stories is the limit for walk-up multiple-access buildings. Taller buildings can be developed with the use of elevators, but the expense of

64
Apartment block, Hamburg. Georg and Michael Wellhausen, 1967.
65
Towers, Vallingby, Sweden. Ancker and Gate, 1953.
66
Apartment blocks, Britz-Buckow-Rudow, Germany. Hannskarl Bandel, 1967.

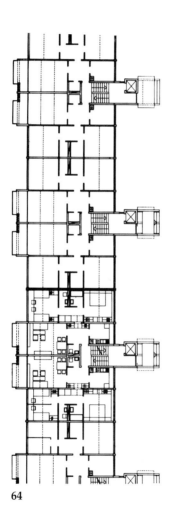

64

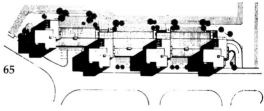

65

repeating elevators is an obvious limitation. Multiple vertical access buildings were very common in Europe before World War II and the subsequent rapid construction of high-rise buildings. Usually, each access stair serves two to four units per floor with semiprivate entrance to each apartment. Since the system permits vertical stacking, it becomes a kind of vertical rowhouse, or rowhouses stacked upon rowhouses. In the United States, where multiple fire exits are required in housing over two floors, this type has never developed. Typical European examples include the Wellhausen project in Hamburg of 1967 (64), where the access core is treated as a separate, external element consisting of a stair for the three-story block and a stair and elevator for the six-story block, and the Candilis, Josic, and Woods walk-ups at Nîmes of 1961 (28), where the stair for a five-story walk-up is the connecting element between apartment blocks, generating a kind of continuous, repetitive building. In the typical housing in Germany of the 1920s and 1930s—Siemensstadt, for example (38)—the access stairs are internal, between units, with only minor articulation indicating the position of the stair on the exterior.

If the vertical access core is greatly extended and centralized, the result is a tower, which may be described as a group of units hooked together along a vertical street. There are countless variations to the tower plan, but it usually consists of several units per floor. Because normally light is required from all sides, a freestanding building (point block) usually results, such as Mies' Lake Shore Drive apartments in Chicago, a twenty-nine story building (7). Sometimes, however, the tower connects to other, lower buildings like the four Ancker and Gate towers at Vallingby (65). At other times the tower is simply multiplied and connected together to form the continuous building type like the Bandel blocks of 1967 (66). Although different types of units may be used with multiple vertical access buildings, the walk-up situation is probably better suited for the double-orientation type, and in this respect it is like a rowhouse. With the tower, the single-orientation unit type is more typical, with a double-orientation, 90° unit at the corner, although again there are countless possible variations.

Corridor Buildings

The term "slab," implying a tall, long building, is commonly used to describe corridor buildings, although a corridor system is not limited to high-rise buildings. Dwelling units in a slab simply align along a continuous corridor that has periodic connections to the ground. Building height and vertical access requirements are a function of building regulations and varying economic considerations such as elevator costs and other mechanical services. However, slab heights vary widely and any optimum condition is more the result of local building conditions.

66

67
Spangen Quarter, Rotterdam. Michiel Brinkman, 1919.
68
Narkomfin Apartments, Moscow. Moses Ginzburg and I. Milinis, 1928.
69
Bergpolder apartments, Rotterdam. Van Tijen, Maaskant, J. A. Brinkman, and van der Vlugt, 1933.

Corridor buildings come in two basic types, single-loaded and double-loaded, and there are many variations of each. Some have corridors every floor, others have corridors every second, third, or even fourth floor. Some have corridors occurring at different positions in the section at different levels.

Single-Loaded Corridor Systems
Buildings of this type generally open to the side away from the corridor and hence are commonly used where there may be a preferred view or orientation or some undesirable site condition that the unit can, in effect, turn its back to. A corridor-every-floor system usually results in a building made up of single-orientation units; an alternating corridor system often results in two-level or maisonette unit types, with both single and double orientation. Where the climate permits, the corridor can remain open (gallery access) and becomes a kind of street in the air, a concept evolved in 1919 by Brinkman in the Spangen Quarter in Rotterdam (67) and employed in postwar English housing such as Park Hill (2). The Narkomfin collective housing project in Moscow by Ginzburg of 1928 (68) is an enclosed version of an alternate-level gallery-access system.

Single-loaded system; corridor every floor. Examples of this type include the Bergpolder slab in Rotterdam of 1933 by the team of van Tijen, Maaskant, J. A. Brinkman, and van der Vlugt (69), a very early experiment in high-rise housing; the Billardon slab at Dijon by Beck of 1954 (56); and Alvar Aalto's apartments at Bremen of 1958 (10).

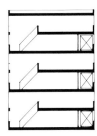

Single-loaded system; corridor every second floor. This popular type was frequently used in postwar, low-rise housing. It consists of maisonettes off an access gallery with bedrooms above, often over the corridor. Stirling and Gowan's Preston housing at Lancashire of 1961 (11) demonstrates the type: three-story buildings with private entrance to a lower level and an access gal-

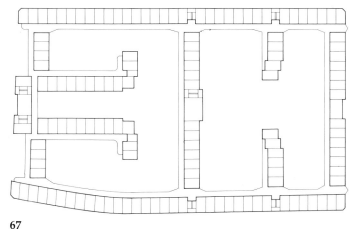

67

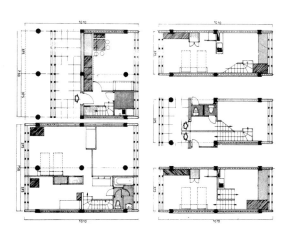

68

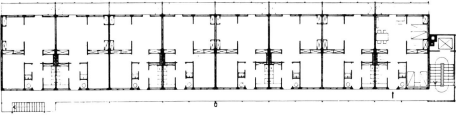

69

70
Rowhouses, Runcorn, England. James Stirling, 1968.
71
El Paraiso apartments, Caracas. Carlos Villaneuva, 1956.

lery for the upper maisonettes. Stirling's Runcorn housing (70) is perhaps an evolutionary development of the same scheme, with the building now five stories high and a gallery at the third floor. Here the maisonette on the bottom two floors has private entrance at ground level, the gallery gives access to the maisonette on the next two floors, and stairs give access to the flat on top, which extends over the gallery. Brinkman's Spangen Quarter (67) is a very early example of this type. Here the gallery, really an independent structure, services upper maisonettes while independent stairs and private entrance give access to the two lower units in a four-story building. Le Corbusier's Immeuble Villas projects (12) are more extravagant: two corridors side by side, one service and one public, give access to a huge two-story unit with a double-height living room and large terrace. The same idea is also used in much taller buildings. For instance, the L'Aero Habitat slab of Bourlier and Ferrier in Algiers of 1950 (51)—a thirteen-story building and a series of slabs, one placed perpendicular to a steep slope—and Villaneuva's El Paraiso slabs in Caracas of 1956 (71).

Single-loaded system; corridor every third floor. The more unusual types of single-loaded, alternate-level corridor buildings position a corridor every third floor with stairs up or down to the units that are not at the corridor level.

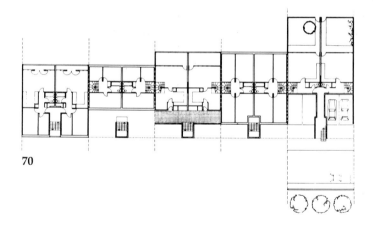

70

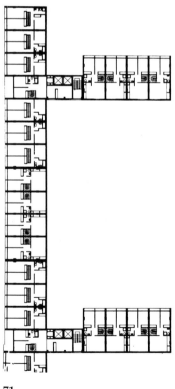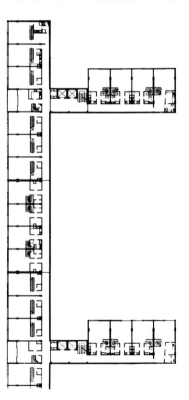

71

72
December Apartments, Caracas. Carlos Villaneuva, 1956.
73
Nytorp apartments, Malmö, Sweden. Jaenecke and Samuelson, 1959.

Sometimes there are maisonettes at the corridor level with a smaller apartment below, sometimes there are larger units below. This is strictly a low-income housing type except where the maisonette is used, and it is typical of high-density, low-income public housing such as Park Hill (2). Slabs with a single-loaded corridor only every fourth floor are quite unusual because few building codes allow such a considerable inconvenience. However, this kind of building is sometimes built in South America; the Villaneuva slab in Caracas, the December Apartments (72), is one example.

Double-Loaded Corridor Systems
Double-loaded corridor slabs are more numerous than the single-loaded type, and a greater variety of types are possible. Able to accommodate either single-orientation units (corridor every floor) or double-orientation units (skip-stop), this building type has much greater flexibility than single-loaded buildings. Le Corbusier's Unité d'Habitation at Marseilles of 1952 (46) popularized the double-loaded, skip-stop section, and it appears frequently thereafter in many countries.

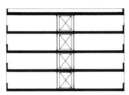

Double-loaded system; corridor every floor. Double-loaded slabs with a corridor every floor are especially sophisticated, popular, and practical in the United States, where fire codes until recently rendered skip-stop systems virtually impossible. This type of building is Mies van der Rohe's stock-in-trade. His Lake Shore apartments in Chicago of 1948 (7) and the apartments in Baltimore (6) are typical and set the pattern for much that was to follow—not only in the organization but also in the image of the expensive, glass-walled residential skyscraper. Although not as popular in Europe, similar types such as the Nytorp slab in Malmö by Jaenecke and Samuelson (73) do on occasion appear.

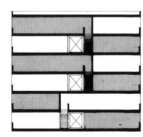

Double-loaded system; corridor every second floor. By far the more common double-loaded types follow the Marseilles Unité example, with corridors every second or third floor. The Lincoln Estate slab by Martin of 1960 in London (5) uses a system of corridors every other floor and an interlocking system of two-level units with living room at corridor level and internal stairs to bedrooms above on the opposite side of the building.

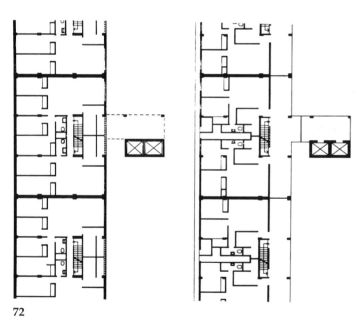

72

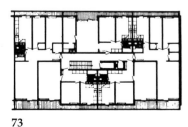

73

74
Unité d'Habitation, Marseilles. Le Corbusier, 1952.
75
Apartment block, Neuwil-Wohlen, Switzerland. Metron, 1962.
76
Apartment block, Munich. Fred Angerer, 1960.

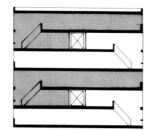

Double-loaded system; corridor every third floor. Le Corbusier's section (74), with corridors every third floor, also uses a system of interlocking units. Unlike Lincoln Estate, however, the living room has a two-story volume and the bedrooms above run through the building. Entrance to one unit is at the living room level and in the other at the balcony level, with the double-orientation part of the apartment below. This is a much-copied scheme; other variations include the Neuwil block (75) by the Metron group of 1962 (although the units here do not interlock) and the Angerer slab at Munich of 1960 (76), a similar type with entrance off the corridor to one unit and stairs to units above and below. Each apartment here, like the Metron slab, is only one floor high. Sert follows this pattern in Peabody Terrace, the married students' housing at Harvard (43), one of the few alternate-level corridor buildings built in the United States until very recently.

Double-Loaded Split-Level Systems
A final variation of the double-loaded corridor system is the split-level type. It comes with corridors every second and third floor or with the corridor in alternating positions in the slab. The idea of the split-level scheme is that one has to climb stairs up or down only one-half level from the corridor. Generally, both single- and double-orientation units are used to get a mix of large and small apartments. The smaller units are usually single-loaded along one side of the corridor while the larger are split-level, usually with sleeping spaces on one side and living area on the other for a double-orientation, dumbbell type.

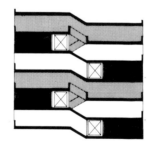

Double-loaded split-level system; corridor every second floor, alternating position. An example of this type is the apartment house in Germany by Schmiedel of 1960 (49), where the corridor is always double-loaded but asymmetrically positioned in section in alternating fashion.

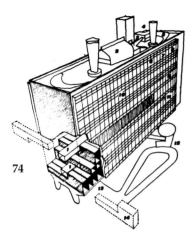

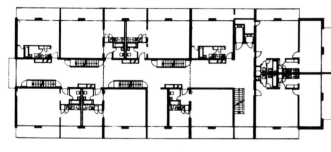

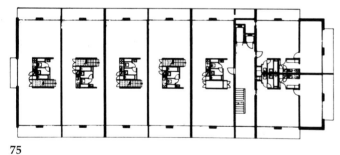

75

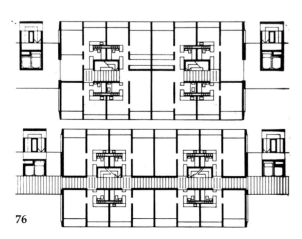

76

77
Ramat Hadar apartments, Haifa. Mansfeld and Calderson, 1964.
78
Apartment slab, Caracas. Carlos Villaneuva, 1956.
79
Apartments, Sausset-les-Pins, France. André Bruyère, 1964.

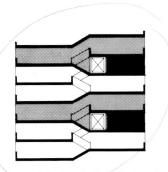

Double-loaded split-level system; corridor every third floor. The Ramat Hadar slab at Haifa by Mansfeld and Calderon (77) is the example of this split-level arrangement, with the corridor always occurring in the same position in section.

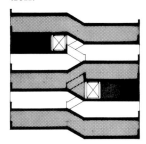

Double-loaded split-level system; corridor every third floor, alternating position. This type became well-known from the van den Broek and Bakema tower at the Hansa project in Berlin in 1956 (50). Villaneuva, however, was proposing the same system at about the same time for a slab project in Caracas (78). The split-level types not only produce very compact buildings with few corridors and minimum walk up or down to each apartment but also create some spatial expansion within the unit because one can see up or down the stairs into opposite halves of the apartment, giving the impression of one large space. The alternating-position corridor scheme also gives larger spaces on one side at each level, thereby accommodating the need to have larger living spaces as well as a mix of unit sizes.

There are countless variations of each typical section. Some buildings would seem to escape classification at all, such as the amorphous group by Bruyère in Sausset-les-Pins of 1964 (79) or Habitat by Moshe Safdie in Montreal of

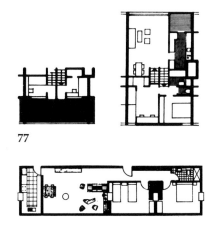

77

78

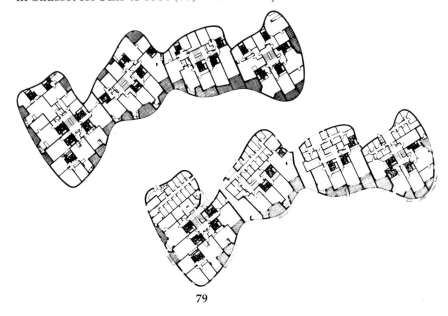

79

80
Habitat, Montreal. Moshe Safdie, 1964.
81
Ziggurat, Israel. Leopold Gerstel, 1964.
82
Durand apartments, Algiers. Le Corbusier, 1933.

1964 (80), which, in its built form, does not seem to exhibit any consistent notion about the combination of units. Still other projects, for instance the Ziggurat in Israel by Gerstel of 1964 (81), do not seem to fit into any building category. Some examples seem bizarre but are really just permutations of stock types. Le Corbusier's Durand project in Algiers of 1933 (82), a strange cantilevered step-section building, is really just a double-loaded corridor, skip-stop type in which units cantilever and diminish in size toward the top of the building; Aalto's tower at Bremen (10), which seems quite unconventional, is just a simple single-loaded corridor plan.

Of the thirty-two case studies that follow, it is significant that only four are from the United States. Two of the four (Suntop and El Pueblo) are groups of semidetached houses of a low-density type, and only two (Peabody Terrace and Price Tower) are high-density projects. Among the more common varieties of urban housing—the rowhouse, party-wall building, blocks, and slabs—no American examples are included; representatives of most of these types can be found, but the choice is limited.

High-density housing in the United States has tended to be either luxury high-rise buildings or racially segregated low-income developments. The luxury housing is publicized and monumentalized (Mies van der Rohe's Lake Shore Drive apartments in Chicago, for example). But more typical has been the Bedford-Stuyvesant/Pruitt-Igoe kind of urban housing—anonymous, overcrowded, racially segregated, and economically depressed. It is doubtful if architecture can ever be the means to social deliverance—the problem is one of national attitudes and policies. Ironically, the dramatic, explosive demolition of the housing slabs in St. Louis (83) happened to buildings which the inhabitants found well designed in some respects but which could not survive an extremely hostile socioeconomic environment. If the Pruitt-Igoe slabs had been built on the outskirts of almost any European city, they probably would have provided useful and acceptable housing.

Americans, with a continent of land available to them, have traditionally taken detached housing as a norm, and until recently a majority of middle-class families have been able to afford it. From 1955 to 1975, however, housing costs rose at almost twice the rate of income;[3] this trend, and the pressures of population growth and fuel shortages, suggest that new housing in decades to come will be preponderantly in forms other than that of the suburban single-family home. If higher-density housing is to become the norm for middle-income families, Americans will find it beneficial to look to a larger international scene for useful housing prototypes. The United States has very few

80

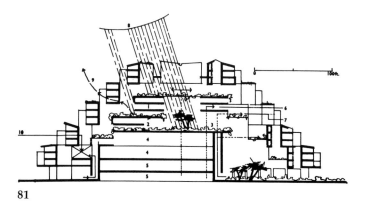

81

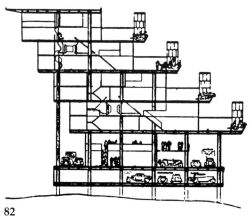

82

Destruction of the Pruitt-Igoe slabs, St. Louis, Missouri, 1972.

that can compare with Spangen Quarter, Siedlung Halen, Frankfurt, or Siemensstadt; and it has had no national housing exhibitions such as Weissenhof or Hansaviertel to which outstanding architects and planners have been invited.

The buildings that follow are presented as case studies of different types of housing from throughout the world, beginning with the lower-density building types and ending with the high-density types. Included are detached housing (excluding the detached single-family house), rowhouses, terrace houses, party-wall housing, large courtyard housing, slabs, and towers. Each project is described in terms of the history of its development and its importance as a housing prototype. They are intended only as a representative sampling; obviously by no means can all the pertinent housing prototypes be covered in thirty-two examples. These particular buildings were chosen because they represent well-known models of a particular housing type—the Unité d'Habitation of Le Corbusier or Siedlung Halen by Atelier 5 for instance—or because they are particularly revealing examples of a type, such as the Vienna Werkbund Exposition rowhouse of Lurçat or Michiel Brinkman's Spangen housing. All of them, in my judgment, reward study.

3. From a report published by the National Association of Home Builders, Washington, D. C., 1975. The NAHB director of economics derived the contents of this report from statistics furnished by the Department of Housing and Urban Development.

83

Detached and Semidetached Housing

Suntop Homes   Frank Lloyd Wright

El Pueblo Ribera Court   Rudolph M. Schindler

Daal en Berg Duplex Houses   Jan Wils

Group of Court Houses   Mies van der Rohe

Kingo Houses   Jørn Utzon

a
Cloverleaf Ground Subdivision, interior perspectives.
Frank Lloyd Wright, project, 1942.
b
Suntop Homes, section.
c
Suntop Homes, exterior view.

Suntop Homes

ARDMORE, PENNSYLVANIA, 1939

Frank Lloyd Wright

The Suntop Homes and Wright's later Cloverleaf Ground Subdivision of 1942 are important attempts to increase the density of a basic suburban housing type, the single-family detached residence. Stylistically and spatially from the same mold as Wright's Usonian houses of this period, Suntop may be thought of as four Usonian houses placed in each quadrant of a cross formed by two perpendicular party walls. The unit in each corner is three floors high; it features ample balcony and terrace space on the upper floors, a carport, double-height living room, private entrance, and a private garden. The idea was to combine four three-bedroom single-family houses while still maintaining the amenities and privacy of the detached single-family residence.

In each unit the living room on the ground floor opens out to the garden. The kitchen and a small dining room occupy the second floor or mezzanine overlooking the double-height living room. The master bedroom and a double-height bathroom are also on the second level. Two small bedrooms are arranged on the third floor, with the remainder of the roof for terrace. The Cloverleaf project—really just a deluxe version of Suntop—has an interior courtyard at the intersection of the party walls, an additional bedroom on the second floor, and another bath on the third floor. The second-floor bath, originally double-height to allow ventilation from the roof, is reduced to one level and vented onto the courtyard. The bedrooms feature balconies on the courtyard side.

a

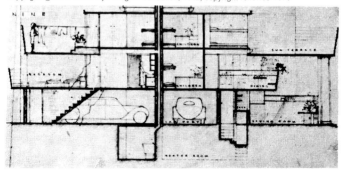

b

c

a
Cloverleaf project, unit plans.
b
Cloverleaf project, perspective.

Suntop presents an interesting prototype for multifamily dwellings in a suburban setting. Only one of the projected four buildings at Ardmore was constructed, however, and the idea has inherent difficulties. First, Wright apparently did not see the space-saving advantage of combining utilities and parking areas: each of the four units has its own heating system and a private garage. Second, in the equal quadrant or pinwheel plan every building has to be approached from four sides and is surrounded by streets that have to be crossed to get elsewhere. As a result, in the Cloverleaf development, a high percentage of the total area is paved to provide access. Another problem with the pinwheel notion is that each building is separate and isolated and cannot be combined with others in any convenient way. There is no economy of multiplication. The site plans are therefore typically unhierarchical: they are made up simply of equally spaced, identical buildings.

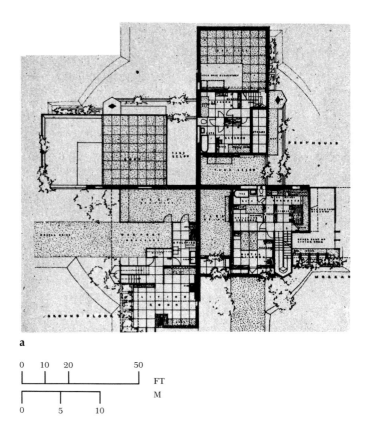

a

0   10   20   50
|————|————|—————————|
                        FT
                        M
|————————|————————|
0   5   10

b

Suntop Homes, axonometric.

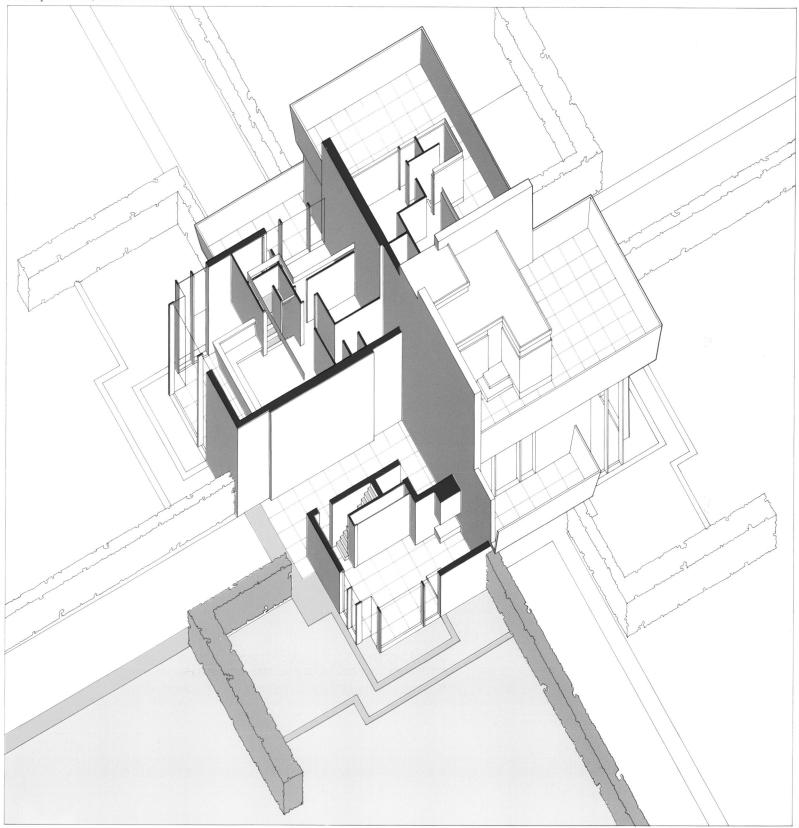

Plate 1

El Pueblo Ribera Court

LA JOLLA, CALIFORNIA, 1923

Rudolph M. Schindler

a

Educated in Vienna and acquainted with the work of Wagner, Hoffmann, the Secessionist architects, and particularly Adolf Loos, Schindler became an early follower of Frank Lloyd Wright. Doubtless familiar with Wright's *Wasmuth* portfolio of 1910, Schindler came to America in 1914 and by 1917 was working for Wright on buildings like the Tokyo Imperial Hotel and the Hollyhock house in Hollywood. He even produced the working drawings for the Millard house in Pasadena, the first of Wright's precast concrete block houses. Intertwined with the impressions derived from this background were others derived from observations of Los Angeles. Thus, in El Pueblo Ribera houses references to Loos and Wright are fairly easy to see, but equally evident are ideas about outdoor living, courtyard or patio houses, and trellised verandas—all benefits of a mild climate—as well as the influence of a local building tradition.

The Lowes house of 1922 at Eagle Rock, designed while Schindler was still in Wright's office, anticipated ideas that were worked out the following year in El Pueblo Ribera Court. The first Lowes project was a stucco building with a very light, airy, wood superstructure of windows and trellises, reminiscent perhaps of the highly articulated upper parts of some of Wright's work. Or possibly the superstructure was simply derived from the Spanish Revival buildings with which southern California abounds, an indigenous architecture of white stucco walls and timber structure with balconies and roof pergolas. The concept of a heavy wall supporting light upper forms may also have been derived from Wright and local sources, but it is important that Schindler himself was experimenting with concrete walls. He knew about Irving Gill's tilt-slab buildings (Schindler built his own house just across the street from Gill's Dodge house of 1916), and in addition to the Millard house he designed the Monolith house with Wright in 1919, both of which have concrete walls. The second scheme for the Lowes house uses slip-form reinforced concrete, the technique employed in El Pueblo Ribera just one year later.

Schindler was very interested in the bungalow courts that became popular in southern California in the second decade of the century. Designed as small vacation cottages near the ocean, El Pueblo Ribera is similar in some respects to Gill's bungalow court projects of this period, the Lewis Courts at Sierra Madre of 1910, and the Horatio West apartments at Santa Monica of 1919. Schindler also designed a bungalow court project for Jacob Korsen in 1921, but the really important precedent for El Pueblo Ribera was the double house that Schindler designed for Clyde Chase and himself in Hollywood in 1922. Two houses, each an L-shape, interlock onto a common kitchen and a guest suite but are rotated ninety degrees so that each opens onto a completely private patio enclosed by the back of one unit and a series of hedges. There are private entrances on each side, resulting in movement through the house from the closed side to the open patio. The plan changed with El Pueblo Ribera from an L to a U, but the effect is the same: private patio with the house opening onto it. Solid walls,

31

El Pueblo Ribera Court, axonometric.

a
El Pueblo Ribera Court, general view.

a

33

a
Monolith Home, perspective. R. M. Schindler and Frank Lloyd Wright, project, 1919.
b
Buck house, plan. R. M. Schindler, Los Angeles, 1934.
c
Schindler residence, plan. R. M. Schindler, Hollywood, 1922.
d
El Pueblo Ribera Court, plan.

sliding wood and glass doors, transom windows, and wooden roof structure constitute an architectural vocabulary shared by both buildings. This is a theme Schindler was to use over and over again in countless variations in both his projects and buildings. The Buck house of 1934, for example, is just a variation of the L or U parti.

El Pueblo Ribera units are U-shaped, with kitchen, bedrooms, and bath in the two smaller side wings and a large central living room in the middle. The side wings protruding past the living room give access to the hedged-in patio. Outside stairs lead to a roof terrace that can be used for sleeping in hot weather. It

a

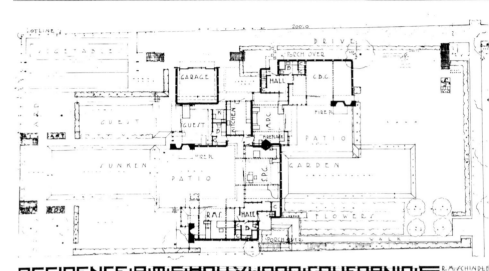

c

b

d

34

a

b

El Pueblo Ribera Court, view from the patio of a typical unit.

is covered with a wooden trellis from which a canvas awning could be suspended, and from the terrace one can view the ocean. The unit was made of slip-formed concrete, over the objections of both the client and the lending institutions—objections that proved to be well-founded, since apparently the roof leaked badly, rendering the unit virtually uninhabitable when it rained. The perimeter concrete wall of each house has few openings on the sides away from the patio. The patio side, however, opens entirely onto this private garden space with operating windows, wood frame sliding glass doors, and transom windows, producing an interior flooded with natural light. The walls at each side of the living room—the intersection of the legs of the U-plan—extend above the top of the perimeter wall and provide support for the roof trellis.

The standard U-shaped unit fits together with other units in a variety of ways, but always the principle of patio privacy is maintained, the backs of adjacent houses or hedges making the necessary enclosure. The site arrange-

a

ment and single-story building height ensure that sunlight reaches every patio space. Parking is provided in common garages, with only a short walk required to any unit.

Although El Pueblo Ribera is basically an organization of detached houses with private yards and private entrances, there is close to fifty percent land coverage and a rather dense population for suburban, single-family living. These are really small vacation houses, but it does not take much imagination to see how they might be transformed into larger units and still maintain all the present amenities. El Pueblo Ribera demonstrates that a suburban lifestyle can be preserved on a fraction of the land area required for the typical house.

a
Huis ter Heide, plan and elevation. Robert van t'Hoff, project, 1914.
b
Cheney house, plan. Frank Lloyd Wright, Oak Park, 1904.
c
Country house of precast concrete, perspective. Jan Wils, project, 1918.
d
"Fireproof House for $5,000," perspective. Wright, project, 1906.

Daal en Berg Duplex Houses

DEN HAAG, 1920

Jan Wils

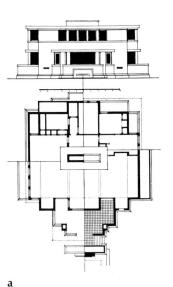

a

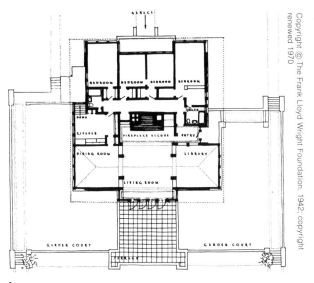

b

c

A founder of the "Stijl" movement (along with Theo van Doesburg, Robert van t'Hoff, and J. J. P. Oud) and later a member of the Dutch Functionalism group of the twenties and thirties, Jan Wils, like Schindler, was an early proponent of Frank Lloyd Wright, whose 1910 portfolio *Wasmuth* influenced many Dutch architects. Both Wils and Robert van t'Hoff had been experimenting with Wrightian notions before the founding of the review *De Stijl* in 1917. Van t'Hoff had seen some of Wright's work in the United States in 1910, and in 1914 he designed a concrete house—Huis ter Heide—which is obviously copied after Wright's early prairie houses but especially resembles the Cheney house of 1904 or the Hunt house of 1907. Like both of these houses, van t'Hoff's house employs a three-part symmetrical plan with porches and a central fireplace. A cruciform organizationally, the building has solid corners and cantilevered roofs. Glass is used symmetrically in the center bay, and planters, porches, and outside walls are treated as extensions of this zone.

Wils, too, was apparently looking closely at Wright. His 1918 country house in precast concrete is nearly identical to Wright's 1906 "Fireproof House for $5,000" or its built version, the Hunt house of 1907. The lateral extension in both cases seems to be an entrance trellis leading to a vertical element that is presumably a stairway. Closed corners, open central bay, and low outlying walls that define the garden or terrace space are part of this vocabulary. Even the rendering of the two houses is similar: the angle of view is nearly the same and the trees are in positions similar to those in the *Wasmuth* perspective.

d

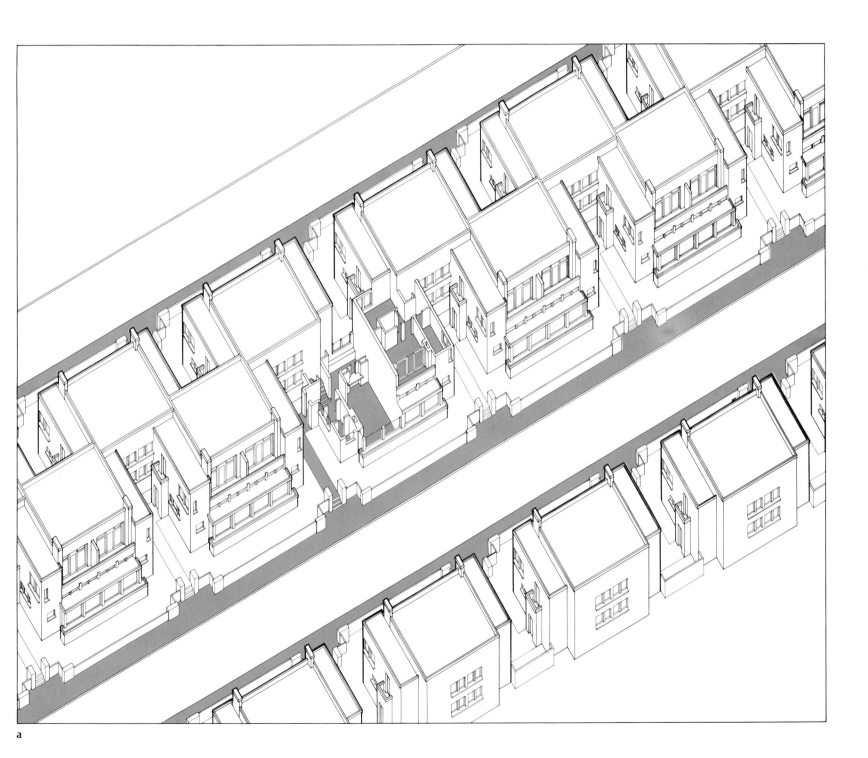

Daal en Berg duplex houses, typical street view.

a

a
Daal en Berg duplex houses, site plan.
b
Daal en Berg duplex houses, unit plans.

The Daal en Berg buildings of 1920 are really just the 1918 concrete houses turned into a group of stucco duplexes. Whereas Wright was dealing mostly with the detached house in a suburban milieu, his Dutch counterpart was dealing with urban apartments. The transformation from detached house to dense duplex was remarkably easy.

The typical building consists of two two-story houses back-to-back, but treated as one building, with living and dining areas, kitchen, and entry below and three bedrooms and a bath above. Entrances and stairs for the two houses are at opposite sides of the building—the equivalent of the solid corner in the Wrightian prototype—so that duplexes can be placed side by side with no loss of privacy or light and air. Entrance is from a small walkway into an entry hall, where stairs and a sitting room with toilet define the solid corner zone. Next is a large living room opening to a front garden separated from the street by a low wall. The living room projects out a few feet from the face of the house, giving access to the garden past the solid corner of the toilet. The kitchen is to the rear, serving a dining area that is spatially part of the living room. Upstairs, three bedrooms are arranged around a central hall and bath; the master bedroom opens to a balcony.

There are two typical site arrangements. First, side-by-side duplexes face the street, with a small entry walk and garden in both front and rear. The second more dense version places duplexes back-to-back in a staggered arrangement, so that the kitchens and upstairs rear bedrooms of the rear building get light from the entry court of the two buildings in the front. From the street this arrangement gives the appearance of one continuous building that steps back to give entrance. The garden wall also steps back to make a gateway with steps up to the entry walk between each duplex.

Duplexes offer obvious advantages for medium-density urban housing. High-rise apartment buildings are usually unattractive for family living because play areas must be detached from the apartment; although the outdoor space for each duplex is not large, there is a private garden or play area with room for large trees and a private entrance. In addition, the placement of living and sleeping quarters on different floors is an advantage in a high-density family situation. The Wils duplexes are highly articulated, architecturally hierarchical, and carefully proportioned—a fine early example of a medium-density housing development in a pleasant urban environment.

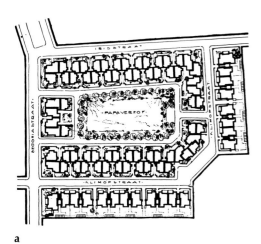

a

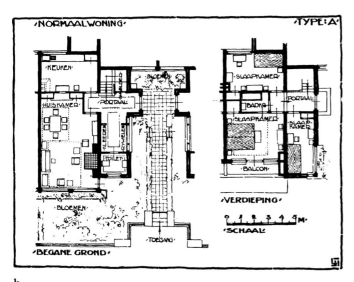

b

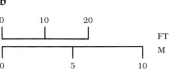

Group of Court Houses
1931

Mies van der Rohe

This project may be thought of as a higher-density version of Mies van der Rohe's earlier detached single-family houses. It utilizes a similar architectural vocabulary of roof plane independently supported on steel columns, floor-to-ceiling glass, and freestanding, sometimes perpendicular, interior walls and service elements that define a plan characterized as "free-flowing"; but the Court Houses, unlike Mies's earlier freestanding projects, are within walled courtyards and thus maintain absolute privacy within the unit. Instead of a suburban pattern of isolated buildings, a continuous texture of housing results —a building mode more suitable to an urban life-style.

Mies's brick house of 1923 is in many ways the forerunner of the later Court Houses project. Like its predecessor, the typical court house consists of a series of masonry walls of constant height extending outward from the interior space of the house. Perpendicular transparent planes of glass connect to these walls and separate internal from external space, though both share common walls. A horizontal roof plane rests on the walls, again providing interior and exterior with a common surface. Later Mies houses—the Wolf house of 1926 and the Herman Lange house of 1928—utilize additional window systems, but they nevertheless represent an architecture of horizontal and vertical masonry planes separated by glass.

In the Barcelona Pavilion of 1929—also a system of perpendicular planes— the roof is supported by a regular grid of composite steel angle columns. Freed of any supportive role, the walls are clearly independent of the structural grid but continue to slide past both internal and external space and to be separated by glass planes. Service elements are also independent of the column grid, and the entire system rests on a definite podium. Although Mies had used a steel-frame system before—in the apartments at the Weissenhof exhibition of 1927 —the free-plan notions at Barcelona are definitely post-Weissenhof phenomena, and one may surmise that Mies's discovery of the liberated-column grid came from Le Corbusier's two buildings at Weissenhof, where exposed composite steel and round columns were used. Most post-1927 Mies buildings (until the Chicago experience, where the column migrates to the edge of the floor slab) employ a "Dom-ino" type of regular structural grid: a cantilever floor slab with the column inside the outside edge of the slab. This can be seen in the Tugendhat house of 1930, the Berlin Exposition house of 1931, the Court House project of 1931, the House with Three Courts of 1934, and the Courtyard Houses of 1938.

The typical unit in the Court House project uses the wall and column combinations of the earlier buildings and is the predecessor of the House with Three Courts. Although there are different unit types—T-plans, L-plans, rectangular plans, some with fireplaces, some with guest houses and pools—all incorporate the basic ideas of the House with Three Courts: regular structural-column grid on a raised gridded podium, a compound totally enclosed by defining walls,

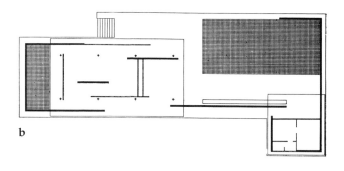

a

b

c

Group of Court Houses, axonometric (hypothetical arrangement).

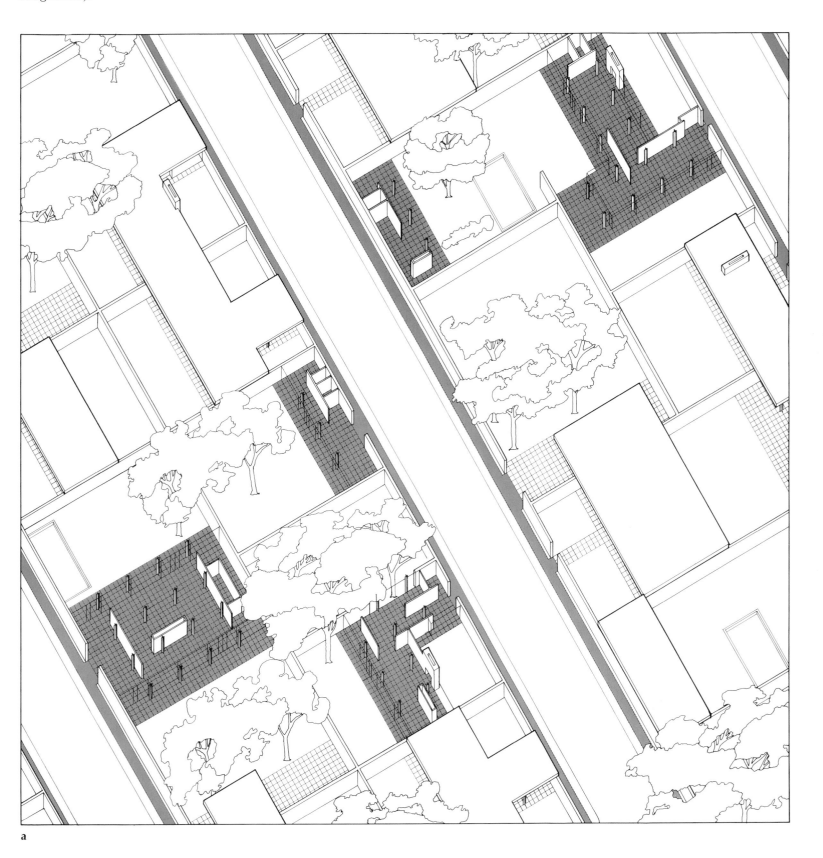

House with Three Courts, plan. Mies van der Rohe, project, 1934.

and a set of hierarchically-sized garden spaces (small for bedrooms, larger for living rooms, and larger still for entry, pool, or guest house).

The typical single-family detached house, set back from the street and away from adjacent houses (as required by most building codes) and arranged so that the major spaces of the house open to a space in front of the house that is not closed off from the street, seems rather at odds with an urban society's need for privacy and security. The Court Houses offer absolute privacy: the space along the street belongs to the house instead of the street through the simple act of enclosing that space within walls. Other advantages include the uncomplicated system of construction, flexibility of size and arrangement, and adaptability to problems of orientation. Although Mies's arrangement here shows a housing pattern of rather low density—usually unsuitable for urban living—it is not difficult to imagine a two-story or duplex version with similar properties of privacy and simple construction but with increased density.

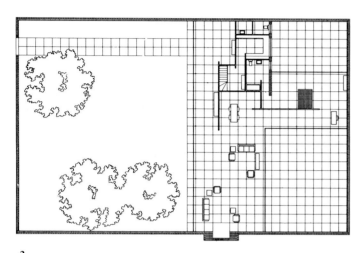

a

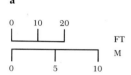

a
Kingo Houses, site plan.
b
Kingo Houses, typical unit plan.

Kingo Houses

ELSINORE, 1956

Jørn Utzon

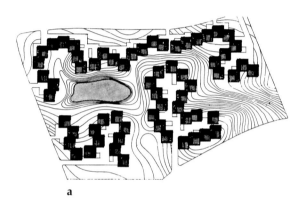

a

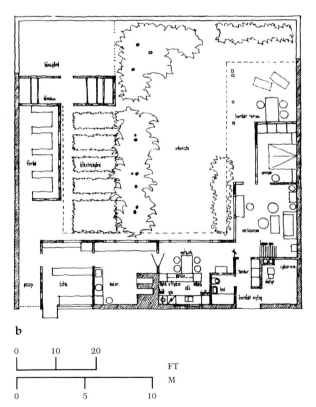

b

```
0      10     20
|__|__|__|__|__|           FT
                           M
|__|__|__|__|__|
0      5      10
```

Building in Denmark has been somewhat outside the European mainstream of modern architecture. At the turn of the century a reaction to industrialization resulted in a bias in favor of national arts and crafts—a form of national romanticism. By the thirties people like Kay Fisker and C. F. Møller were making reference to the International Style in their Copenhagen housing projects: long, low-rise, garden apartments with balconies and shops below. But many of the wartime and postwar architects abandoned any International Style overtones and reverted to a kind of arts and crafts version of housing, in which apartments were made to appear to be detached, freestanding single-family houses with steep sloping roofs and brick detail. Arne Jacobsen probably brought full-blown International Style architecture to Denmark with his glass and steel corporate buildings such as the SAS air terminal in Copenhagen of the early fifties. However, he remained in touch with the arts and crafts movement, and the worldwide popularity of "Danish Modern" in the fifties can perhaps be traced to Jacobsen's furniture and the famous "egg" chairs. This national handicraft tradition was manifest in Jacobsen's buildings as well. His Klampenborg terrace houses of 1950 seem to refer back to a traditional Danish architecture: brick buildings with sloping tile roofs and chimneys, with external spaces that are clearly defined and enclosed but arranged with a very open relation to nature in mind.

This combination of modern and traditional vocabulary seems to be a part of Utzon's architecture as well. Although probably eschewing the Bauhaus reference that Jacobsen might have made and clearly rejecting the rather parochial brand of national housing characteristic of postwar Denmark, Utzon still looks at traditional notions through the eyes of a modernist. His own house of 1952, a long, low, frame building with brick walls and expansive glass privately ensconced in a forest clearing, is but a modern version of the traditional Danish farmhouse—rectangular, brick, sprawling, but cozy.

Similarly, the Elsinore project of 1956 and the court houses at Fredensborg of 1962 attempt to fuse modern needs with traditional ideas. Sixty-three separate houses are grouped together on a gently undulating site. Consolidated to achieve common automobile access, collective open space, and building economy, the farmhouse—with its sloping tile roof, dominant chimney, and same-sized windows—has here been transformed to meet a modern need. The resulting irregular site plan establishes several different typical orientations and building connections. Houses are arranged in a loose group with restricted access for the car and an entry on one side; the other side opens to a pond, a slope, or some other aspect of a very picturesque setting. A more or less random grouping results, but the impression is of repetitive units.

Although there are several different plans, each house has a courtyard about 50 feet square that is defined by a brick wall. Attached to two walls of the court and opening onto it is an L-shaped house; a tile roof slopes from the top

a

a

Kingo Houses, typical section.

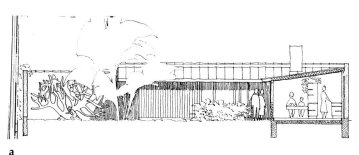

of the wall down to the house's inside edge. Entry is usually into the intersection of the legs of the L, with dining and living spaces in one direction, bedrooms in the other. Variations include garages, studio or workshop spaces, or simply sheds attached to other sides of the court—endless do-it-yourself additions seem possible. Similarly, the courtyard space itself can be varied in many ways: paving, vegetable gardens, large trees. The exterior wall is high enough to give ample slope to the roof while still allowing adequate depth and height to the interior rooms. Where there is no adjacent building, the wall is lower to give views or access to the open parts of the site. The exterior wall is interrupted only by small windows for the kitchen or baths; the garden side of each house is mostly glazed, however, orienting the unit in that direction. Overall consistency is maintained by the repetition of brick, higher chimneys, and tile, which appears not only on the roofs but as coping on walls and chimney tops as well. Constant slope on roofs and copings adds another note of consistency.

Although the plan of each house is clear, the organization of the site seems random; relationships to other buildings do not seem specific, and it is probably significant that the later project at Fredensborg incorporated a community center—a gesture to community life that the Kingo Houses could not claim. Though they were isolated in the countryside—an Utzon preference—the court houses would seem to be an even more useful urban housing prototype. Absolute privacy is guaranteed and each is a very secure, self-contained living environment. Perhaps derived from Jacobsen's Klampenborg project, the Kingo Houses offer most of the advantages of suburban living, including complete privacy, but on about half the area.

Rowhousing

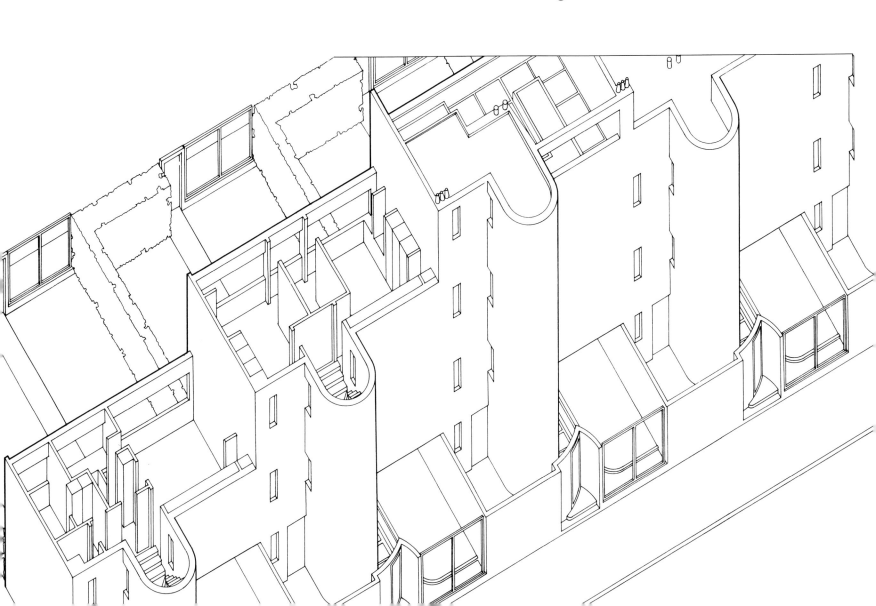

Weissenhof exhibition apartment house, axonometric.
Mies van der Rohe, Stuttgart, 1927.

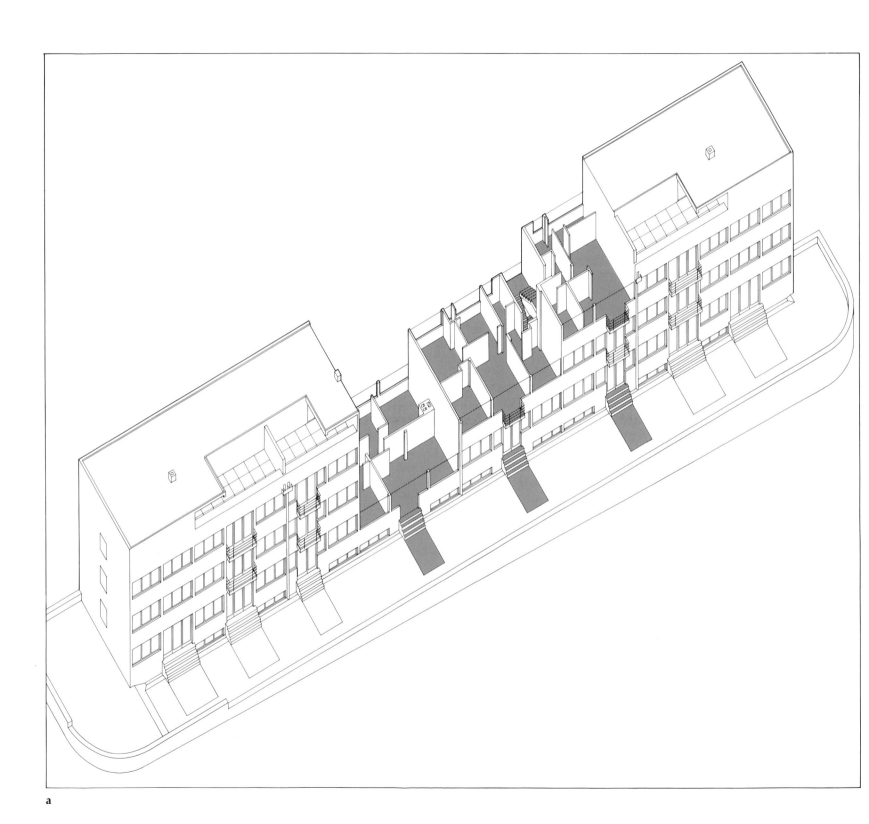

a

Apartment House

WEISSENHOF EXHIBITION, STUTTGART, 1927

Mies van der Rohe

Mies brought together a remarkable international group of young architects at the Weissenhofsiedlung, an exposition originally conceived as several serpentine terraces of more or less continuous buildings of similar height, following the contours of the site. The version that was later built was changed to an arrangement of freestanding buildings still on the slope and following the contours but discontinuous and of varying heights. Including the work of Gropius, Le Corbusier, Hilberseimer, the Taut brothers, Hans Scharoun, J. J. P. Oud, Mart Stam, and others, the completed project exhibited a remarkable stylistic consistency and clearly established what Hitchcock was later to name the "International Style."

The Mies apartment house is by far the largest building in the group, its size further accentuated by its dominant position at the top of the slope. This was one of the few plots level enough to easily accommodate a long, continuous-height building. Four floors high with the top floor given over to washrooms and terrace, the building is arranged around four internal sets of stairs that serve two apartments per floor. A variety of one-, two-, and three-bedroom units face the street on one side and on the other open to a narrow garden partly enclosed with a low wall. This facade is more open, with stairs leading down to the garden. The frame construction is readily apparent on both elevations. Although the frame is in the outside wall and therefore regularly interrupts that surface, a definite horizontal effect is created with large strip windows between the frame on both sides of the building. The terrace on the garden side opens to the other buildings and the view of the valley below.

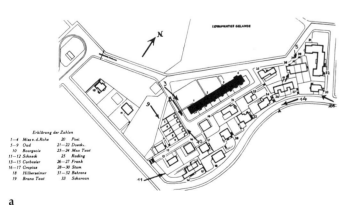

a

b

51

a
Weissenhof exhibition, aerial oblique of completed project.
b
Weissenhof exhibition apartment house, plans. Mies van der Rohe.

a

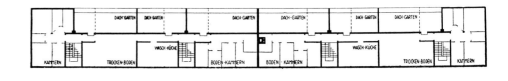

b

This apartment building may have been the prototype for the large housing projects that sprang up all over Germany during the 1930s—long, continuous buildings with walk-up units arranged around internal stairs. They were white stucco with flat roofs, minimum detail, strip windows, and usually either balconies or, as with Stuttgart, roof terraces and some kind of garden space. The Weissenhof project was probably not subject to the same economic and programmatic specifications as the typical *siedlung* of the years following, and consequently the size and variety of units in this building were not typical of later municipal housing projects. Still, the building was viewed as a low-cost prototype, and standardization and prefabrication were major considerations. It is notable that Mies was able to maintain a sense of proportion and elegance of detail that, although usual for him, was not typical of later projects. In housing construction in Germany the popularization of the International Style after Stuttgart was synonymous with a vulgarization of detail, and rarely were the many projects of the next decade able to match the spaciousness and sophistication of the Stuttgart apartments.

a
Weissenhof exhibition, site plan (J. J. P. Oud's buildings indicated).
b
Kiefhoek rowhouses, typical unit plans. J. J. P. Oud, Rotterdam, 1925.
c
Weissenhof exhibition rowhouses, typical unit plans. J. J. P. Oud.

Rowhouses

WEISSENHOF EXHIBITION, STUTTGART, 1927

J. J. P. Oud

J. J. P. Oud and Mart Stam were the only Dutch architects to participate in the Stuttgart exhibition. Although there was considerable variety in the apartments designed by different architects for Weissenhof, the Stam and Oud projects were quite similar to Oud's earlier work: the 1924 rowhouses in the Hook of Holland and the 1925 Kiefhoek project in Rotterdam. Like them, Weissenhof consists of two-story, repetitive rowhouses with entrance gateways on the street and small gardens behind. Although the Stuttgart apartments have entrance courtyards with a utility wing on the front and a full bath upstairs and feature larger kitchens, they are still basically like the typical Kiefhoek unit, with its living room and kitchen below and three small bedrooms above. The continuous surface of the street side at Kiefhoek has given way to the highly concatenated elevation of Weissenhof, with its utility blocks and entrance gates projecting out from the main volume of the building and a more distinct definition of each house. This causes some problems because the main entrance from the street is into the courtyard and then into the kitchen, while the living room faces the garden—the reverse of Kiefhoek.

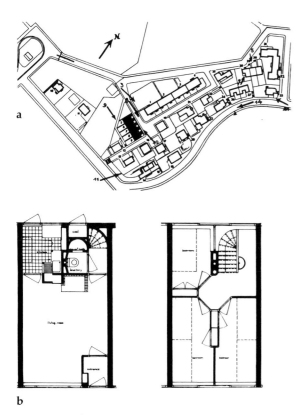

a

b

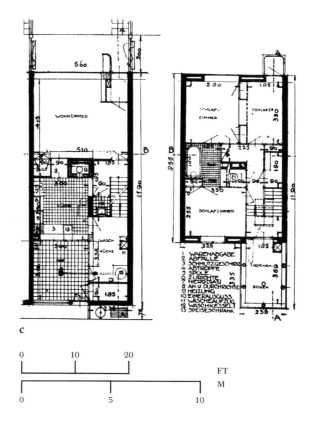

c

0   10   20   FT

0   5   10   M

54

Weissenhof exhibition rowhouses, axonometric.
J. J. P. Oud.

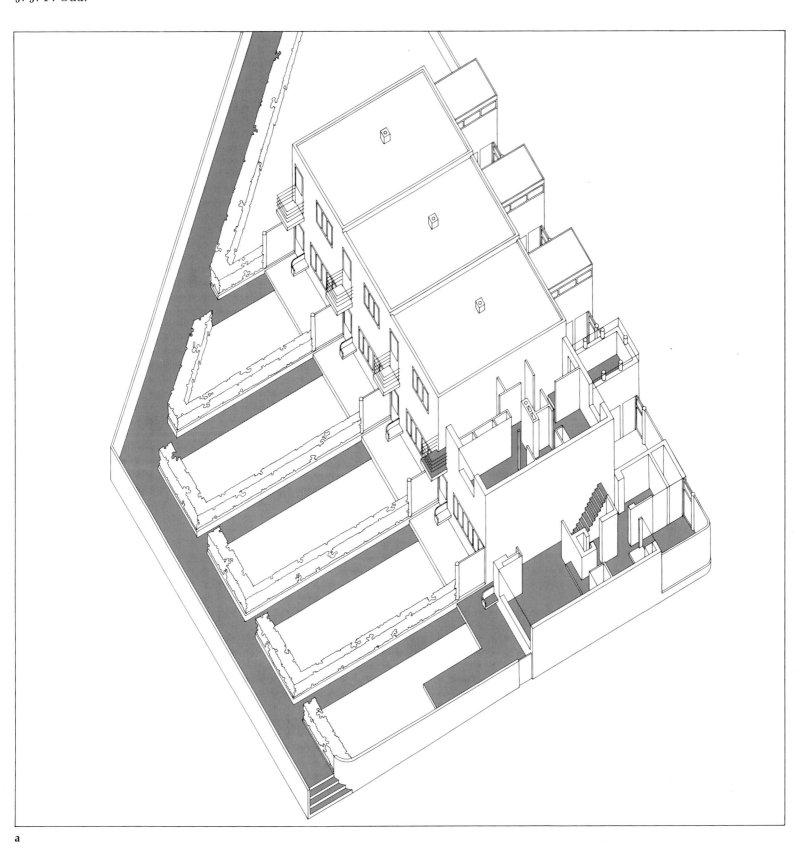

a
Weissenhof exhibition rowhouses, view of entrance side.
J. J. P. Oud.

Although the details changed somewhat, both projects were the typical Dutch workers' housing of the time—two-story, white stucco units with small rooms and minimum services. Compared to the rather extravagant projects of Mies van der Rohe and Le Corbusier at Weissenhof, the Oud rowhouses are unpretentious, very clean, and simple—a straightforward solution to the problem of low-income housing.

a

a
Vienna Werkbund Exposition, site plan (André Lurçat's buildings indicated).
b
Vienna Werkbund Exposition rowhouses, view of entrance side. André Lurçat.
c
Vienna Werkbund Exposition rowhouses, garden elevation. André Lurçat.
d
Vienna Werkbund Exposition rowhouses, floor plan. André Lurçat.

Rowhouses
WERKBUND EXPOSITION, VIENNA, 1932

André Lurçat

The Austrian version of the Weissenhof exhibition, the Vienna Werkbund Exposition, brought together a second generation of International Style architects as well as the older members of the Vienna School, Josef Hoffmann and Adolf Loos. Typical of the experimental housing expositions of the period, the Vienna project consisted of twenty-seven separate buildings scattered rather randomly on a flat, triangular site and containing a total of seventy different apartments of varying design and size.

The Lurçat scheme consists of four three-story rowhouses and is an important prototype for dense, low-rise urban housing. The typical unit faces the street with an almost blank wall, a walled-in entrance court with a recessed gateway, and a rounded stair tower, also blank, attached to the solid main block. The opposite side, which faces a small garden, is very open, with strip windows and a breezeway from the entrance court. The ground floor, aside from the main entrance into the stair leading to the living areas above, contains the utility functions. This service level is clearly established in elevation by the height of the courtyard wall on the street and by the clerestory windows on the garden side. The second level consists of a living room, dining room, kitchen, small bath, and small bedroom. Above are two larger bedrooms and on top, as a variation of the prototype, a roof terrace opening to the garden side.

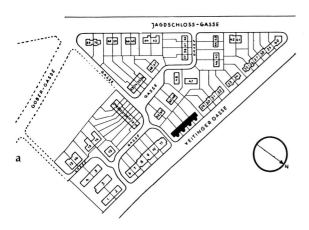

a

b

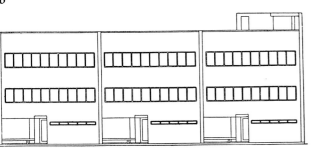

c

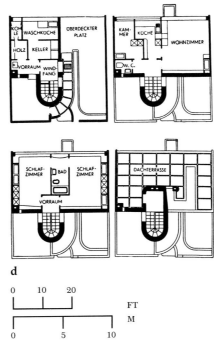

d

0   10   20

FT

M

0   5   10

Probably the most outstanding building of the exhibition, the Lurçat houses are clean and simple but at the same time are unique for several reasons. The usual party-wall rowhouse is narrow and long—a depth of about 40 feet—and is plagued by dark interior spaces. Lurçat here developed a very narrow unit that can go on a shallow lot (the usual rowhouse requires a deep lot); all rooms are amply lit and most are the depth of the building. The stairs that come forward from the surface of the building provide both needed articulation to the usually monotonous rowhouse elevation and a large-scale element that makes the building suitable for a variety of urban needs. Another innovation is the walled-in entrance courtyard, which offers private space on the street side of the building and a transition between the street and the living areas. The wall and gateway also help to enliven the elevation. The design allows room for considerable flexibility. The roof terrace could easily become another bedroom or studio and the breezeway could become another room or, indeed, the ground floor could become a separate apartment. This adaptability to changing needs and family size makes the Lurçat project a particularly attractive solution to present housing problems.

Vienna Werkbund Exposition rowhouses, axonometric
(hypothetical extension). André Lurçat.

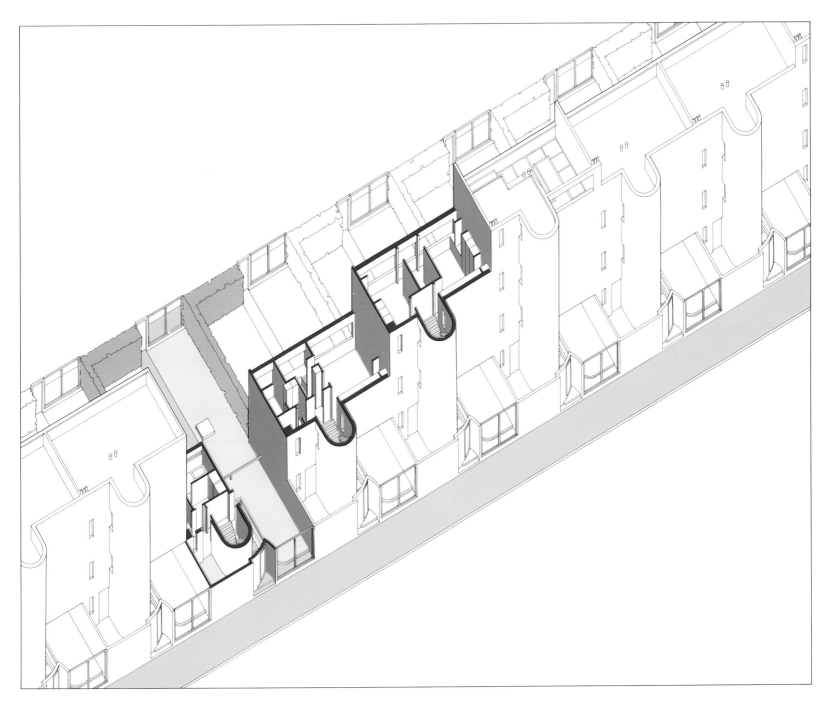

Plate 2

a
Ichinomiya rowhouses, site plan.
b
Ichinomiya rowhouses, two-story-unit plan (left), one-story-unit plan (right).

Rowhouses
ICHINOMIYA, 1961

Kenzo Tange and Urtec

The Western world has for centuries turned to rowhouses for urban living. They are quasi-communal, share walls, are more or less identical, and are two-sided, that is, they face a street on one side and open out to a garden on the other. In the East this has not been the common housing form, even in a dense urban context. The typical building was the single-family house within a walled compound, with entrance through the courtyard or garden—a closed rather than communal system.

The Ichinomiya group represents the Eastern equivalent of the rowhouse. It is in a rural setting not unlike dense European housing estates such as Sied-lung Halen—it is a sort of miniature Halen set aside in the Japanese country-side. Although the individual units are much smaller than their Western counterparts, the grouping is rather typical of Western arrangements. The landscape plays a much more dominant role, however, and the buildings rather easily accommodate themselves to the existing stream and trees. There is still evidence of the traditional building form, the building in a compound. The project has been divided up into smaller districts by the use of high stone walls that describe a precinct or neighborhood of twenty to thirty one- and two-story units arranged loosely around an open space or play area. Each unit has a garden defined by a low wall, and a higher wall separates every second unit. The gardens here are used to grow vegetables rather than to extend the living space.

There are several different types of units. Built on a module of about 11 feet, the one-story units use two bays—about 23 feet—and the two-story units only one bay. Both types are of comparable size, about 400 square feet, with four rooms each. Only the two-story apartments have balconies, but both have a paved patio on the garden side. Two units share a service wall that contains

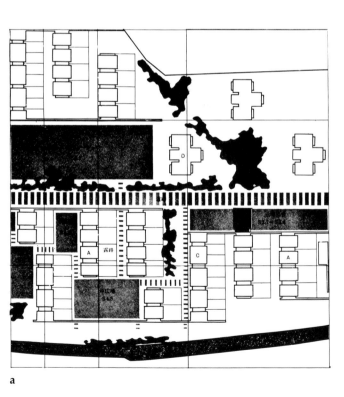

a

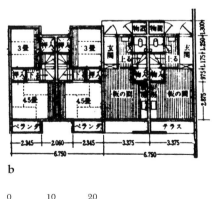
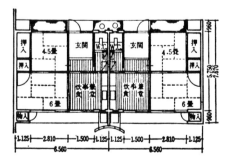

b

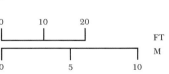

```
0        10       20
                        FT
                        M
0          5        10
```

59

Ichinomiya rowhouses, axonometric.

the cooking facilities, minimum bath, and stairs. The lower floor of the two-story unit is the living area, and sleeping quarters are above. The one-story units are divided into four parts consisting of living and dining areas and two sleeping rooms. The service zone in each type is articulated by a panel that comes forward of the main block and contains a utility wash area. This zone also has a lower roof height. The building material is concrete, with contrasting field stone for the high compound walls.

Though small by Western standards, the Ichinomiya group is interesting and attractive. A dense, repetitive housing form has been achieved at the expense of some privacy, although each apartment still has an enclosed garden and balconies and the neighborhood is defined by the larger walls. In typical Japanese fashion, the landscape has been manipulated with apparent ease, and Western planners would do well to carefully observe the results.

a

a
Siedlung Halen, site plan.
b
Siedlung Halen, house plan.
c
Siedlung Halen, aerial view.

Siedlung Halen
BERN, 1959–1961

Atelier 5

Coming at a time when the design of housing was particularly problematic—high-rise urban buildings were not satisfactory for family living and suburban housing was uninteresting and too sparse—Halen seemed to offer a sensible alternative that combined many of the best features of both urban and suburban living. It is a dense, repetitive, communal, multistory project, but at the same time it is isolated in a picturesque country setting with the sun, the trees, and fresh air. It offers absolute individual privacy and private ownership—the presumed amenities of the suburban life-style.

Halen is uniquely located. Although only three kilometers from the center of Bern, its physical separation is guaranteed by the existence of a municipal woods between the site and the city. Halen consists of eighty-one terrace houses arranged in two staggered rows on a sloping site. Built on a condominium principle, the houses are individually owned but the land and all the group facilities, such as the garage, swimming pool, heating plant, club, and laundry, are collectively owned. The units are highly repetitive but there is still great variety. Types range from studio units with small gardens to seven-room houses, some with additional studios. Most of the houses are three-story units of four, five, and six rooms arranged on the slope, with entrance at an intermediate level from a public pedestrian street. The two main types differ basically in the position of the staircase. In one type the stair is perpendicular to the long axis of the house, and in the other, the stair is parallel to the long axis. Nearly every bedroom and living area opens onto a completely private outdoor space, and kitchens typically open to a courtyard directly off the entrance to each unit.

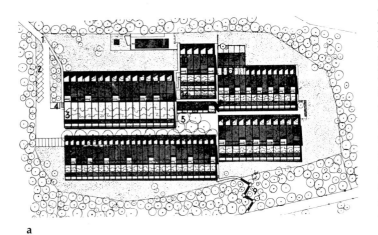

a

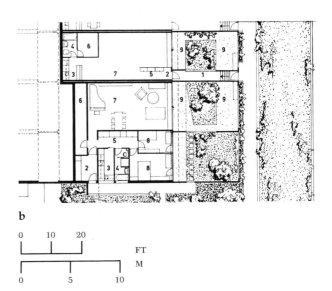

b

```
0    10    20
|----|----|         FT
                    M
|----|----|
0    5    10
```

c

Siedlung Halen, view from the south.

a

Siedlung Halen, axonometric.

Plate 3

a
Siedlung Halen, type 380 house and studio, plans and section.

Halen has been criticized as being too obviously an eclectic version of the La Sainte Baum and Roq and Rob projects of Le Corbusier. This may be so; however, the idea of the long slot of space also comes from a typical Swiss building form, the medieval houses of Bern, and Halen is really a modern interpretation of this design. Halen has also been criticized as being somehow artificial in its setting and too small to really function as the independent community it appears to be. Nevertheless, Halen has certainly set the standard for the design of dense, individual houses in a communal context without the sacrifice of individual privacy. Although the setting is rural, Halen is potentially an urban building form: the standards of privacy are a function not of the suburban site but rather of careful unit design and arrangement. Halen probably has been singularly influential as the model of high-density, low-rise housing in the Western world.

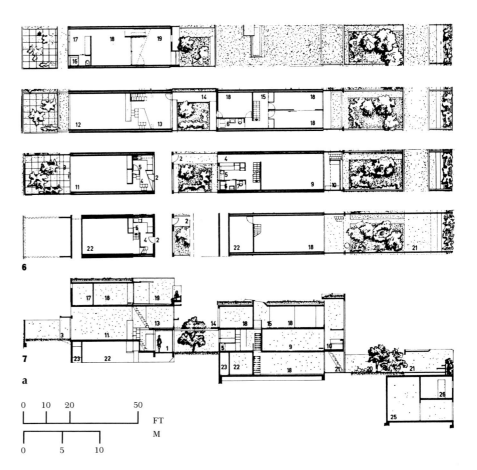

65

a
Typical Bedford Square house, plans and section.
b
Fleet Road terrace housing, site plan.

Fleet Road Terrace Housing

LONDON, 1967

Neave Brown

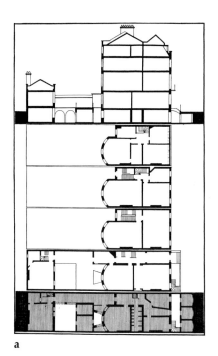

a

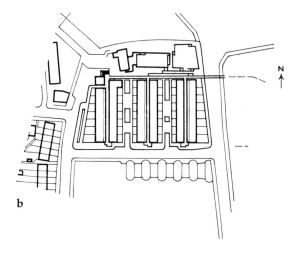

b

Postwar housing in London was frequently a mixture of high-rise slabs or towers and rowhouses usually scattered loosely about the larger buildings. This pattern was begun with the Highpoint blocks by the Tecton group in 1933 and dominated most housing development after about 1947. Examples include Churchill Gardens by Powell and Moya (1947), the Golden Lane estate by Chamberlin, Powell, and Bon (1953), and the Roehampton and Alton estates done by teams of architects for the London County Council (1953). Many of the building and urban ideas applied in these projects were derived from Le Corbusier's great theoretical works of the twenties and thirties, Plan Voisin and La Ville Radieuse, which established a precedent for building large towers and slabs that are freestanding in spaces carved from the existing city.

Criticism of this pattern of housing was widespread, centering on sociological facts and realistic observations about the nature of urban change. Family living in high-rise buildings was a problem in spite of the seductive images of rooftop nursery school playgrounds, running tracks, and buildings that stood freely in undefiled green countryside—images created by Le Corbusier's Unité d'Habitation at Marseilles. Other criticism, perhaps more important, drew attention to the effect of this kind of building pattern on the "physique" of the city. A skeptical attitude was emerging about an urbanism that was destructive of the existing urban fabric. Traditionally, housing in the city formed a more or less neutral background of repetitive buildings, a texture that was accentuated by a city's special institutions and public buildings. Although the "redent" blocks of Le Corbusier's Ville Radieuse conformed to this tradition, it was the tall buildings, the towers of Plan Voisin and the Unité at Marseilles, that became the prototypes for much of the housing that was to inundate postwar London.

The most common form of housing in London was the terrace house, the English equivalent of the rowhouse. Usually a three- or four-story party-wall structure, the terrace house was set back a few feet from the sidewalk by steps and small gardens in front and another behind, and established a continuous surface along the street. The larger terrace houses were serviced from the rear by an alley called the "mews," which also gave access to the stables along the alley. Typically, there were small apartments above the stables or garages, a row of buildings that was gradually converted to residential use. The resulting pattern was parallel rows of housing with open space between. The buildings to one side were usually larger and taller than the others, and each unit opened to a small, private outdoor space.

Access to the terrace house was up a few steps from the street to the front door and entrance hall. Although there were many plan variations, in most cases the living room fronted the street and a large combination kitchen and dining area opened to the rear garden. The stair from the entrance hall led to the bedrooms on one or two levels above. A basement on the half-level below

a
Typical site arrangement of terrace houses, London.
b
Fleet Road terrace housing, five-person-unit plans.
c
Fleet Road terrace housing, two- and four-person-unit plans.

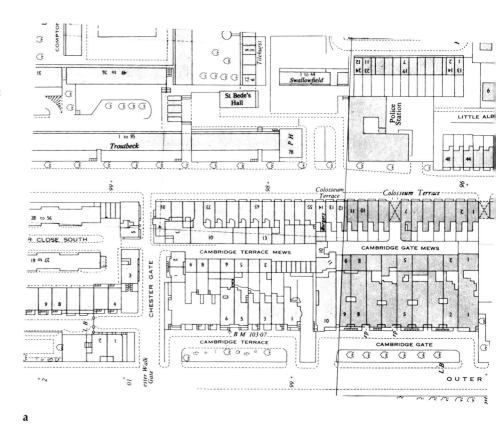

a

b

c

| 0 | 10 | 20 | | FT |
| 0 | 5 | 10 | | M |

Fleet Road terrace housing, general view.

a

the street was often leased as a separate apartment, reached by a stair from the sidewalk that led down to a private entrance. The resulting open zone between the front of the building and the sidewalk also had many variations, but usually doubled as a modest front garden and a source of light for the lower apartment.

The split-level, multiunit section and the parallel rows of low buildings are characteristics that the Fleet Road project shares with the typical London terrace house. Neave Brown has also adopted the additional features of a large

a

a
Winscombe Street houses, plans. Neave Brown, London, 1966.
b
Fleet Road terrace housing, section.

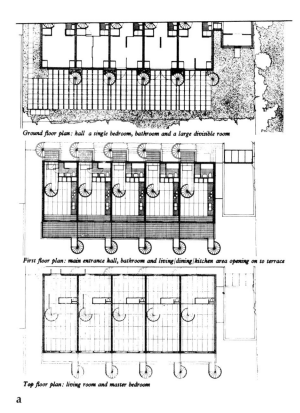

Ground floor plan: hall a single bedroom, bathroom and a large divisible room

First floor plan: main entrance hall, bathroom and living/dining/kitchen area opening on to terrace

Top floor plan: living room and master bedroom

a

two-story unit or maisonette above, small one-floor unit or flat below, balconies above, terraces below, and a narrow space providing entrance to the lower units. Indeed, Fleet Road is simply a smaller, modern version of the terrace house, with integral parking below.

Set into a neighborhood of intersecting streets and existing buildings, including a four-story sea cadets' training center, Fleet Road combines about seventy units into six two- and three-story, parallel rows of terrace apartments. Sets of two rows of units are serviced from a central pedestrian walkway. The three-story row contains two-story, three-bedroom maisonettes on top and one-bedroom flats below. The top floor of the maisonette, the living room area, opens to a balcony, while the entry level connects across the walkway to a semiprivate terrace on the roof of the apartment on the opposite side. Access to the one-bedroom units below is from the walkway. These lower apartments open directly to private courtyards either at grade or on top of the adjacent parking structure. The lower walkway is open except where the bridges above cross to the terraces, allowing light to penetrate down to the lower level. The two-bedroom unit is a split-level variation of the one-bedroom unit, with entrance at grade to the kitchen and with stairs up half a level to the bedrooms and down half a level to the living room, which also opens to a private courtyard.

The plan, peculiar to the terrace house, that makes the dining area part of an enlarged kitchen has been incorporated into Fleet Road, although the living room has been moved to the upper level of the maisonette to form an adult suite with the master bedroom. This is a strategy that Neave Brown also employed in 1966 with his own houses at 19 Winscombe Street.

Fleet Road is an important prototype because it demonstrates that a high-density form of housing with outdoor space for each dwelling can be achieved without giving up individual privacy. This project may be seen as a modern version of an existing, traditional form of housing—the terrace house—designed to be a discrete, ameliorative insertion achieved without the destruction of the urban housing fabric that accompanied so much housing construction of the past thirty years. Although Fleet Road was preceded by other examples of high-density, low-rise housing such as the Amis, Howell, Killick, and Partridge rowhouses in Hampstead of 1956 and Brown's Winscombe Street houses, this project was significant as a model for the return to a more traditional building form as the basic housing type.

a

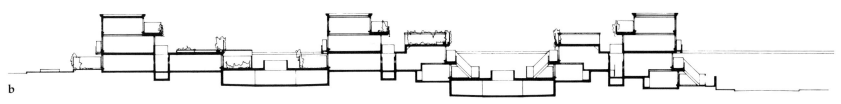

b

Party-Wall Housing

25 bis Rue Franklin Apartments Auguste Perret

Avenue de Versailles Apartments Jean Ginsberg

Porte Molitor Apartments Le Corbusier

Casa Rustici Lingeri and Terragni

Parklaan Apartments W. van Tijen

Rue Franklin Apartments, axonometric.

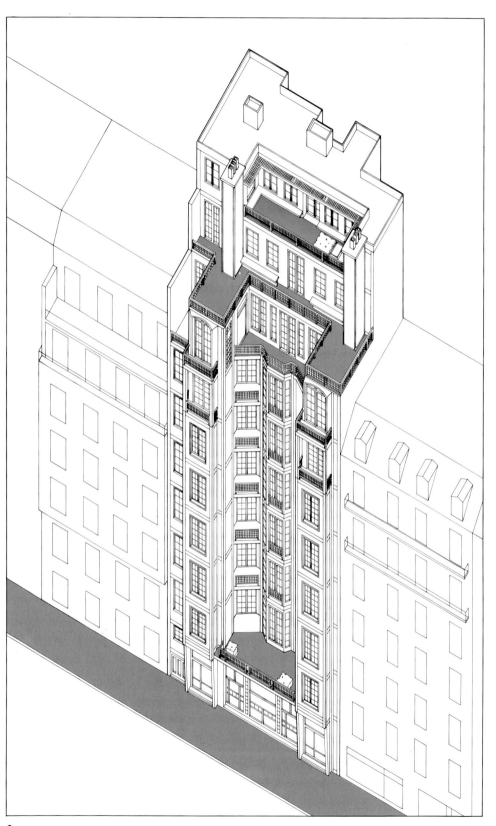

a

74

25 bis Rue Franklin Apartments

PARIS, 1903

Auguste Perret

Although Perret's early masterpiece has been much discussed as the first building to really express an architecture of reinforced concrete, it is perhaps more important as the first clear application of the technology of modern architecture—here the reinforced concrete frame—to a traditional housing type, the party-wall townhouse. An extension of the nineteenth-century fondness for art nouveau decoration, neoclassical symmetry, and commercial iron building details, the Franklin Apartments are nevertheless a precursor of modern architectural tastes. Perret inventions such as the exposed frame, glass block, flat roofs and roof terraces, flush glass detailing, and a very open plan that can only be thought of as the predecessor of the free plan quite obviously excited the following generation of architects. And although Le Corbusier, who worked in the Perret atelier in 1908 and 1909, would not have liked to credit Perret with the idea, obviously the Franklin Apartments conjured up fantasies of buildings set off the ground on columns, of freestanding towers (possible with a reinforced concrete frame), of cafés on flat roofs, and of cities that were built upon a grid of concrete piles and would house all of the services of urban life. It is a short step indeed from the pipe rails and terrace planters of Rue Franklin to the roof gardens of the *Oeuvre complète*.

Perret carried on the Parisian tradition of shops below and elaborate roof structure above, but he probably introduced several new variations to the theme. In his version, the shops incorporated two floors, becoming a two-story-high space with a mezzanine level (this was Perret's office and another Corbusian adoption); elaborate penthouse apartments above opened to terraces as the building stepped back for the top three floors. The floors above the street were treated much like typical Parisian masonry construction of the period, although there are cues to the concrete frame within. The surface consists of windows as punctures in the wall, implying that the wall is load-bearing. However, the masonry wall dissolves at the top, exposing the frame, and at the bottom the wall becomes a glass surface.

The building is U-shaped in plan with stairs, elevators, and toilets at the rear wall so that each room has a window to the street. Glass block in the stairway allows light to penetrate while maintaining privacy. On a typical floor there is one large (almost 2,000 square feet) apartment backed up against the service wall. It is arranged around a central, symmetrical suite of rooms—living, dining, and parlor—with kitchen connecting to the service stair on one side and a hallway and one bedroom on the other. The second bedroom adjoins the central spaces at the kitchen side. Both dining area and parlor open to small balconies. Although the plan is very open—a benefit of the rigid frame—it still follows French tradition and is a very rational, comfortable arrangement with separate access to bedrooms, service, and baths and an *enfilade* arrangement in the major suite of rooms.

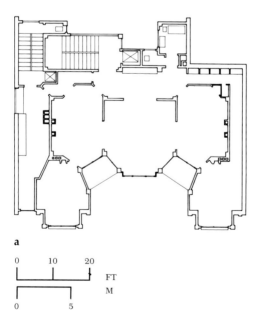

a

```
0        10       20
|    |    |    |         FT
                        M
0             5
```

a
a
Rue Franklin Apartments, detail.
b
Rue Franklin Apartments, detail.

a

b

Rue Franklin Apartments, view from street.

a

While out of the mainstream of modern architecture, Perret's building was certainly seminal for the following generation of architects. The typical apartment is very large even for luxury housing, but it displays many ideas and features that make it a viable modern prototype. Perret has given us a building with considerable depth that does not sacrifice any space to a windowless interior. Because all rooms face the front and because access and services fall in a zone to the rear, lateral extension is feasible and a single-loaded slab with undulating surface could result. As a party-wall type the large flexible plan could easily be reinterpreted as two two-bedroom units of reasonable size. Also, it is not difficult to imagine its transformation into a tower open on one, two, or three sides and even a flip version, a tower with a central core. Whatever the interpretation, the Rue Franklin Apartments inspire sophisticated notions of what housing in cities could be like.

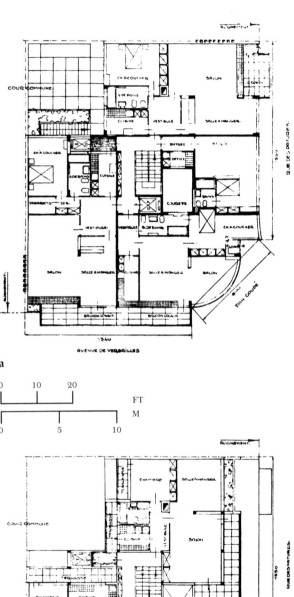

a

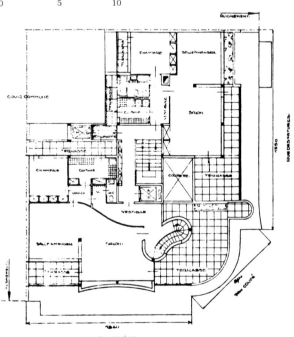

b

Avenue de Versailles Apartments

PARIS, 1934

Jean Ginsberg

Individual party-wall townhouses are of two different types: the double-orientation, open-ended unit, which is adjacent to a building on both sides and faces front and rear, and the double-orientation, 90° unit on a corner, which faces two streets, front and side. Prototypes can be found for each, but the corner site, although less common and perhaps more ambiguous because it faces two streets more or less equally, offers clear advantages. When party walls are at right angles to each other, exterior surface is greatly increased and most rooms can now open to a preferred side, with service concentrated at the interior corner. Multiple-unit versions of this building type give all apartments a frontward organization.

Fronting a major avenue, avenue de Versailles, and a minor street, rue des Patures, Ginsberg's block makes a useful commentary on the corner apartment building. At first glance the rounded corner suggests that any preference for avenue over street was simply ignored. A closer look, however, reveals that although the building presents a frontal and planar appearance to both sides, the avenue side is made dominant through the use of cantilevered balconies; a blank curving wall in the main space of the penthouse apartment on this side axially reinforces this dominance. By contrast, the windows on the street side are flush and smooth, and balcony and penthouse detail are lacking.

In plan the strategy has been to extend the party-wall condition from each side toward the corner, creating two open-ended party-wall units. A 90° one-bedroom unit and a studio are inserted into the front corner of the building. A large courtyard introduced at the inside rear corner gives light and air to the interior bedrooms and also provides service to the rear of each of the open-ended units. One central stair, elevator, and hallway give access to all apartments and together with the baths and kitchens form a central service core within the building.

In section six typical floors are sandwiched between the ground floor (with entrance at the corner) and the elaborate three-story penthouse apartment at the top. After the seventh floor the building volume begins to step back from both streets, forming terraces for the penthouse apartments. The stair connecting the levels of the penthouse continues the strategy of rounded elements at the corner.

Although the individual apartments in this building are dissimilar and hardly prototypical, the more general features of entry floor below, penthouse above with repeating apartments in between, and the unique building itself, are quite prototypical. Ginsberg's skill at packing the corner, at making connection to adjacent buildings, at piecing together a strip-window vocabulary with balconies and terraces, and his sophisticated reference to avenue de Versailles as the dominant street, constitute a remarkable ability to resolve one of the most difficult of building problems: the corner party-wall site.

79

a
Avenue de Versailles apartments, avenue de Versailles
facade.

a

Avenue de Versailles apartments, rue des Patures facade.

a

Avenue de Versailles apartments, axonometric.

a

a
Porte Molitor apartments, typical floor plan.
b
Porte Molitor apartments, penthouse plan.

Porte Molitor Apartments

PARIS, 1933

Le Corbusier

Continuing a tradition of Parisian party-wall townhouses, the Porte Molitor building where Le Corbusier lived is perhaps less important as a housing prototype than as a repository of Corbusian ideas about architecture. Although the building displays much that was evolving in Le Corbusier's oeuvre, it remains an ambiguous building, being perhaps the most experimental of his famous housing projects. Still, Porte Molitor is an important building, even as an experiment, and reference to it can hardly be avoided since there is not a lot of modern party-wall housing—despite its being a traditional urban building form.

Like most party-wall buildings in Paris, Porte Molitor is open front and rear and has a special arrangement on the first and last floors: Le Corbusier's apartment and studio at the top and the main entrance, concierge apartment, and service entrance at the bottom. Whereas most party-wall sites face a street on one side and either a rear garden or a service alley on the other so that there is a distinctly preferential condition, here the building faces a street on each side. In response to this there are two apartments to the typical floor, one facing in each direction, with service walls and stairs on the interior, where a large lightwell brings natural light to the entry and baths of each unit and a small lightwell with service balcony provides access to each kitchen. The penthouse takes up the whole floor, having the studio and a small bedroom at one end and living spaces at the other. On the roof is another bedroom with bath and a terrace. One enters the building through a skylighted lobby. Also at street level are the concierge apartment with private entrance, the service entrance along one side of the service stair, the service elevator, and the servants' rooms at the rear of the building. A ramp from the rear gives access to a modest garage below, where there are more servants' rooms lighted from the rear street by a narrow lightwell. In spite of the small size (about 600 square feet), the apartments are exceedingly generous and convenient: two bedrooms, two or three baths, either a balcony or continuous sliding windows along the outside surface, and a service system that is completely discrete, with servants' quarters connecting via service stair and elevator through the rear of each apartment.

Le Corbusier's free plan, so precious and regular in previous buildings, here becomes a warped single row of irregularly spaced columns, still freestanding but supporting beams that are also supported by the walls on each side. The curving entry wall facing the main lightwell in each apartment recalls earlier themes of rotund shapes played against regular containers. Porte Molitor could be construed to be a party-wall version of the first design for the La Roche house, although that particular curve could very well have been derived from the bend of the chaise longue of 1927—a curve that softened in the famous bathroom chaise longue in Villa Savoye of 1929, became larger for the interior glass wall of the library in the Swiss Pavilion of 1930, and appeared elsewhere as the roof section of Maison Errazuris (1930), and Maison Mathes

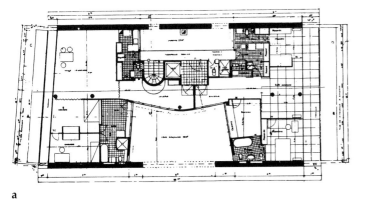

a

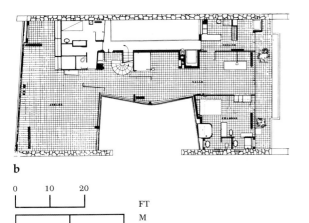

b

```
0    10   20
|----|----|        FT
                   M
|----|----|
0    5    10
```

Porte Molitor apartments, entrance facade.

a

a
La Roche house, first project, plan. Le Corbusier, Paris, 1923.
b
Chaise longue. Le Corbusier, 1929.
c
Swiss Pavilion, plan. Le Corbusier, Paris, 1930.
d
Porte Molitor apartments, detail.

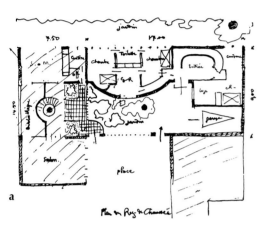

a

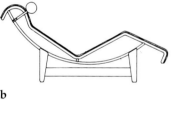

b

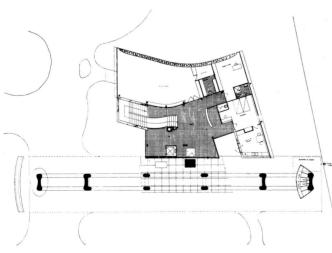

c

(1935), and probably ended up as the major wall at Ronchamp (1950). Other idealized notions of Mediterranean villas made of white plaster with vaulted roofs and rough stone walls are evident. The Corbusian penthouse might even be thought of as a Mediterranean villa attached to the top of a more or less conventional townhouse. The plaster and stone preference, doubtless generated during Le Corbusier's early travels, probably first appears in the house on the lake at Vevey (1925) and continues with Maison Errazuris and Villa Mandrot (1930). Even the Swiss Pavilion uses the rubble-wall theme, and it is continued beyond Porte Molitor in Maison Mathes, Maison de Weekend (1935), and in Ronchamp, where the idea was that the new building should be made from the stone rubble of the old.

Similarly, the vault theme is not new. The very early projects of 1920 and 1922, Maison Monol and Maison d'Artiste, use this Mediterranean theme, and like them the Porte Molitor penthouse vault springs from a wide horizontal lintel, implying a box with the vault as an added element. The vault can be found in Maison de Weekend, Roq and Rob (1949), and in a kind of brutalized brick version at Jaoul (1952) and the Sarabhai house (1955). Unlike all these vaults, however, the Porte Molitor vaults run perpendicular to the side walls, a curious inversion. The idea of the vaulted top for large buildings is another theme occurring later in the Retenanstalt office building of 1933 and in the Immeuble of the Co-op village project of 1934. The Unité at Marseilles has a vault on top and even Ronchamp and the Millowner's Building at Ahmedabad and the Governor's Palace at Chandigarh may be but versions of the type.

While the penthouse is a whitewashed, rubble-walled, vaulted, rustic villa, the rest of the building is pure machine age, with steel and glass walls, sliding doors, steel pipe rails, glass block, and all the other stock Corbusian paraphernalia of the period. The precedents here are also easily pursued. The glass wall is from Immeuble Clarté (1932), with translucent lower panes that align with the railing height (only sliding windows have been replaced with sliding doors). Glass block possibly from Clarté via Cité de Refuge (1932) is used, but there is some speculation that Le Corbusier got this idea from the Maison de Verre by Pierre Chareau, which was completed by the end of 1931 and which Le Corbusier is said to have visited frequently. But then Le Corbusier worked

d

a
Maison de Verre, garden facade. Pierre Chareau and Bernard Bijvoet, Paris, 1930.
b
Porte Molitor, detail.

for Perret for fifteen months and must have seen the glass block in the stairway of the 1903 Rue Franklin Apartments. It is possible, too, that the metal framing of Maison de Verre influenced the design of Porte Molitor; it displays similar modular propensities.

Although Porte Molitor is an adaptive building type—that is, a new building inserted into an existing milieu—Le Corbusier probably saw in it ideal and prototypical urban possibilities. From the windows one can see a stadium in a park, the kind of view Le Corbusier no doubt envisaged for the Immeuble and Plan Voisin projects of the 1920s and later for the Unité d'Habitation: buildings raised off the ground (Porte Molitor's freestanding column at the entrance implies a pilotis system) and freestanding in a park reserved for the athletic activities required of the Corbusian man. The perspective of the facade in the first scheme for Porte Molitor suggests a staggered plan with apartments arranged side by side rather than front and rear. A very similar facade reappears for the Rue Fabert apartments of 1938 in Paris, which are two-level units with entry, dining, and living spaces below and bedrooms above, a two-story-high space in the living area, and access from an interior vestibule. It is a short step from here to the Unité section—an idea that was just possibly developing as early as 1933 in Porte Molitor.

a

b

Porte Molitor, axonometric.

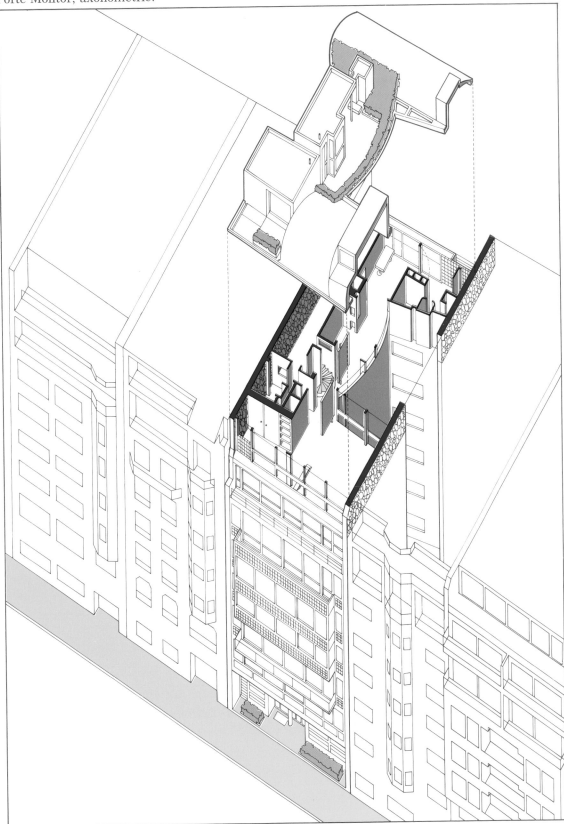

Plate 4

a
Casa Rustici, ground floor plan (top), typical floor plan (bottom).
b
Casa Rustici, detail.

Casa Rustici

MILAN, 1936–1937

Pietro Lingeri and Giuseppe Terragni

The first of the apartment blocks built in Milan by Lingeri and Terragni, Casa Rustici is basically a modern adaptation of the traditional Italian courtyard or palazzo building, but without the disadvantage of a small, poorly lighted cortile. It is made up of two parallel slabs connected by transparent balconies that maintain the surface continuity of the facade on the street while permitting light to enter the large, open courtyard.

Originally the building was to have been a two-story villa, but the owner was persuaded to put the villa on top in the form of a large penthouse apartment. Professional apartments occupy the floors below, with business offices on the ground floor and garage and services in the basement. The owner's penthouse consists of a bedroom wing and a living and dining room wing connected by a bridge. Both wings of the penthouse open to generous terraces.

Access is from the street up a flight of steps to the courtyard level and then into the stair and elevator core in each wing. On every floor a service balcony opens to the court, which is partially covered with a glass block ceiling. Other balconies open from some of the bedrooms both to the courtyard and to the outside of each wing; the connecting balconies on the street side open from the living rooms.

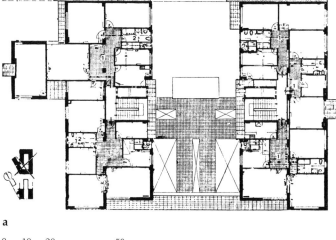

a

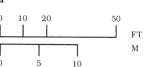

b

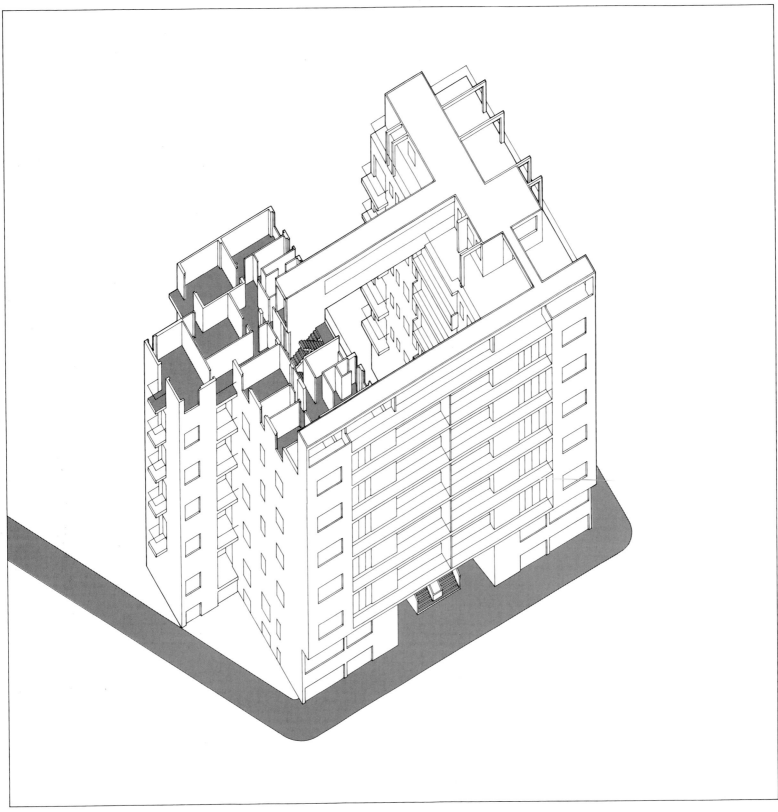

a
Casa Rustici, perspective.
b
Casa Rustici, street facade.

a

b

a
Casa Rustici, street facade.

Casa Rustici is a highly inventive solution to the problem of designing a modern apartment building on a site surrounded by a traditional building form. The site is too deep and too wide for a single slab and the decision to put two parallel slabs perpendicular to the street and connect them with balconies so as to be able to maintain a surface along the street has resulted in an economical and attractive design. Because of the unity given by the balconies, the street elevation is probably more successful than the rather literal expression of the structural frame on the other elevations. Although the palazzo type is usually thought of as a party-wall type—a building that abuts buildings on two sides—Casa Rustici occupies a corner site and opens to three sides. Still, the courtyard is large enough and open enough that the plan could be easily adapted to the typical party-wall situation.

a

Parklaan Apartments

ROTTERDAM, 1933

W. van Tijen

One of the few Dutch architects who was able to maintain continuity in his work before and after World War II was van Tijen, certainly a principal figure in the development of modern architecture in the Netherlands. Surrounded by fine early housing projects such as Michiel Brinkman's Spangen project of 1919 and J. J. P. Oud's Kiefhoek estate of 1928 and inspired by such exceptional modern buildings in Rotterdam as the Van Nelle Factory by J. A. Brinkman and van der Vlugt of 1928, a group of young architects including van Tijen, J. B. Bakema, and van den Broek set about establishing Rotterdam as a center of housing construction in the decade preceding World War II. Removed from the immediate influence of older masters such as Berlage in Amsterdam and from the *Wendingen* group and the expressionistic Amsterdam School, these young architects proceeded to design and build a surprising set of buildings. Because their work was the result of a rational process—simple, straightforward, and without formal preconception—it was immediately labeled "Functionalism."

The Parklaan Apartments are situated on a narrow corner site that fronts a wide, divided, tree-lined, quiet street. They share a party-wall with the next building on the park side but are separated from the building on the other side by an access drive to the garage. An early example of steel frame construction in Rotterdam, the seven-story building, because of its narrow plan, its height as compared to the lower adjacent buildings, and the fact that it is detached on three sides, gives the impression of a freestanding tower.

Although the short side of the building faces the major street and entrance is from the minor street, the building's frontal relation to Parklaan is clearly established by a garden set back from the street and a cantilevered, metal-

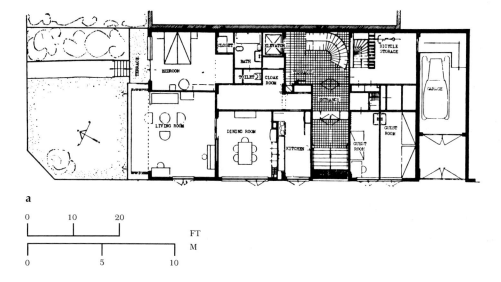

a

```
0     10      20
|__|__|__|__|
                    FT
                    M
0          5          10
|_____|_____|
```

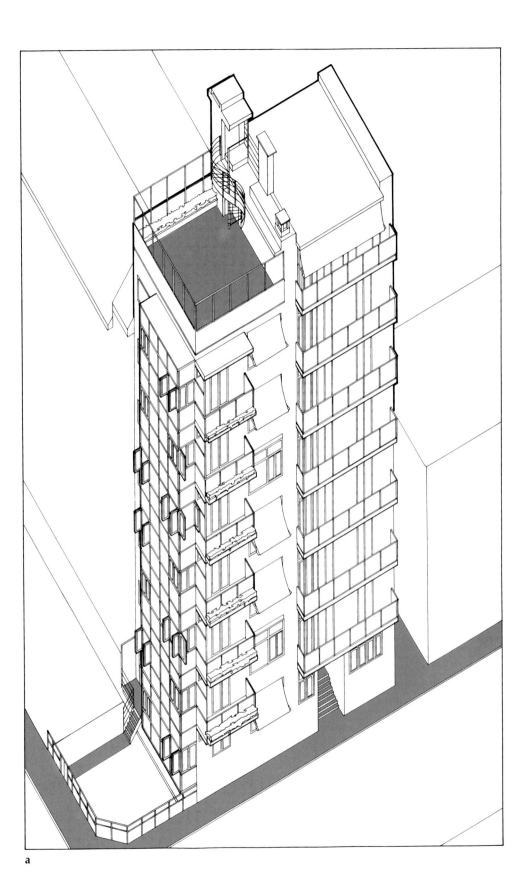

a

paneled extension to the living spaces on this side. Two very modest one- or two-bedroom apartments on each typical floor open to small balconies along the side street and back up to a tight service core and a central stair and elevator. Entrance at the ground level is into a small vestibule, with a one-bedroom apartment opening to the garden space in front and a garage and service quarters in the rear. There is only one apartment at the top, leaving a large, fenced-in roof terrace from which the harbor of Rotterdam can be seen over the rooftops.

Roll-down awnings and a balcony overhang protect the glass from the south sun and enhance the appearance of a lightweight construction. The cantilevered portions of the building, with the glass and metal panels in front and metal balustrades on the balconies, also clearly express the lightness of the steel framing. The generous use of glass and operating windows—a Dutch tradition—creates sunny, airy interiors and anticipates the curtain wall, which appeared in a full-blown version one year later in the "Bergpolder" steel frame slab, also in Rotterdam, done with J. A. Brinkman and van der Vlugt. It is a ten-story, gallery-access slab version of the Parklaan tower.

a

Block Housing

Immeuble Villas   Le Corbusier

Spangen Quarter   Michiel Brinkman

Nirwana Apartments   Johannes Duiker

Hansaviertel Apartments   Alvar Aalto

a
Immeuble Villas, axonometric.

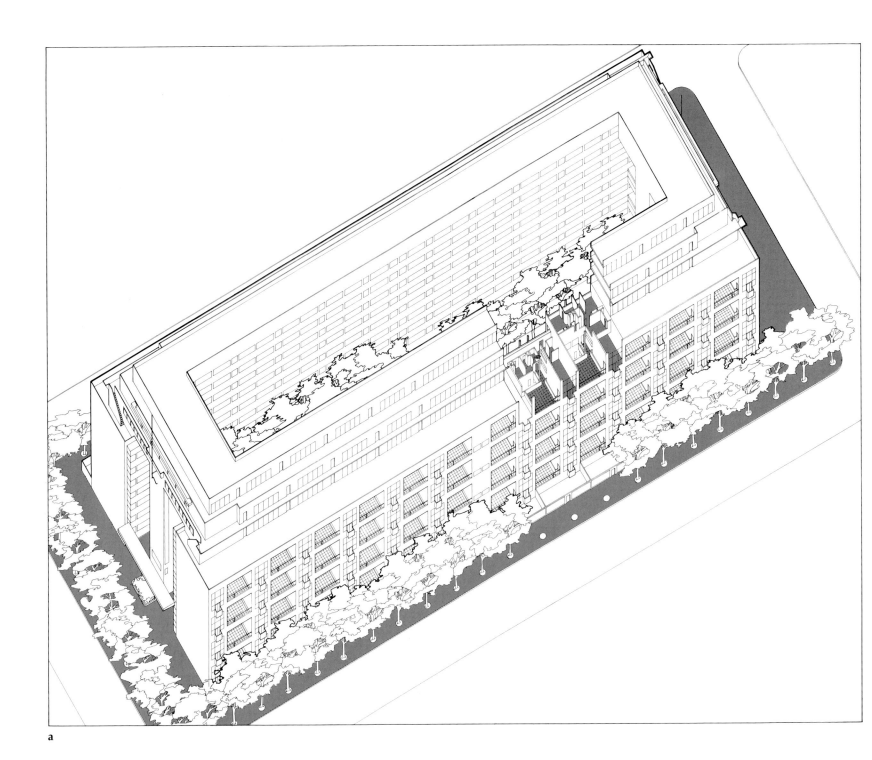

a

Immeuble Villas

PARIS, 1922–1929

Le Corbusier

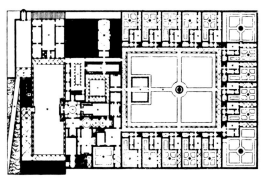

a

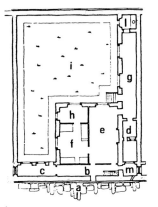

b

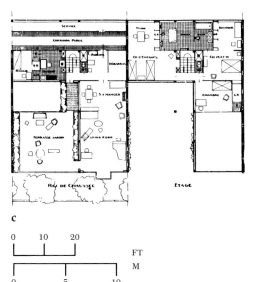

c

Le Corbusier credits the development of the Immeuble Villas unit, actually built as a prototype in the Pavillon de l'Esprit Nouveau in the Paris International Exposition of 1925, to his observations of the Carthusian monastery near Florence, the Certosa di Firenze or Certosa di Ema. The monks' quarters there consist of small walled-in houses arranged around a cloister. Each house is two stories high and opens to an enclosed L-shaped garden. The Corbusian version of this arrangement uses a form of the same approximate dimensions —roughly square and two stories high. However, the house has been extended to include the small porches, so that it is now an L-shaped solid and the garden a cubic void. Access is from a corridor on the courtyard side of the building, an arrangement approximating the cloister loggia of the monastery. Even with these changes, however, the division of the square is the same: the dimensions are almost exactly alike and both are two stories high. The overall building configuration is also similar: identical units arranged around the periphery of a courtyard with communal functions located elsewhere—on the roof of the Immeuble and near the church in the monastery.

The Immeuble Villas (Le Corbusier's term for an apartment building composed of multistory villas) were never built aside from the Pavillon de l'Esprit Nouveau, but the basic notion of an L-shaped solid arranged around a cubic

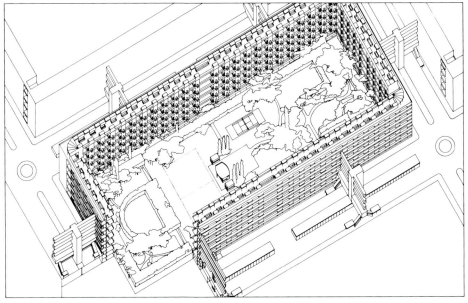

d

97

a
City for three million inhabitants, plan. Le Corbusier, project, 1922.
b
Immeuble Villas, floor plan.

void was a common theme both before and after the pavilion was built. There are elements of the idea in the Citrohan projects, the Ozenfant studio, Villa Meyer, Maison Cook, the garden side of Villa Garche, and Villa Savoye. Even the typical Unité apartment is a variation of the theme. It is obvious why none of the Immeuble projects were actually built. Although suitable for detached and expensive villas such as Meyer or Savoye, the Immeuble unit was certainly less practical in large apartment blocks. The typical three-bedroom Immeuble unit was huge, almost 4,000 square feet, 2,500 square feet of which was actual living area. With a double-height garden of 700 square feet, a double-height living room, a maid's room, double baths, exercise room, and separate service and public corridors, the Immeuble was wonderfully extravagant and, ironically, incompatible with an image of public housing as being economical because it could be mass-produced.

Le Corbusier's observations about urban development are equally important as a source of ideas leading eventually to the development of the Immeuble Villas. Partly the concept stems from Ebenezer Howard's garden city, an idea with which Le Corbusier disagreed but which he transformed into a horizontal garden city with public gardens in the center of each rectangular block and hanging gardens (the terrace) within the unit. Much of the Immeuble Villas notion probably also comes from Tony Garnier and his project Cité Industrielle. Le Corbusier adopted many of Garnier's ideas, and indeed some of the early projects like Maisons Dom-ino and the Troyes project of 1919 even look like typical Cité Industrielle scenes. The Ville Contemporaine, for example, is really just a three-million-inhabitant version of Cité Industrielle, with clear public and private zones, a simple street network, surrounding garden space, and large residential blocks similar to the Immeuble blocks of the Ville Contemporaine.

The Immeuble Villas concept underwent many transformations. This building type and its variants were one of the basic building blocks in a pattern of urban development that evolved from the Ville Contemporaine, Plan Voison, and Ville Radieuse projects of the twenties to the planned reconstruction of Saint Dié of 1945 and ultimately to the Unités of the fifties and sixties. The large rectangular blocks of Ville Contemporaine and the Immeuble Villas projects of 1922 and 1925 were adopted in Plan Voison and Ville Radieuse to become a continuous building that undulated to form larger and smaller spaces and were spread as a kind of uniform texture between large public buildings. The typical unit at Pessac in 1923 was basically an Immeuble type, as was the solid block studio version, the student housing project for the University of Paris in 1925. Still other variations include the Wanner project, the

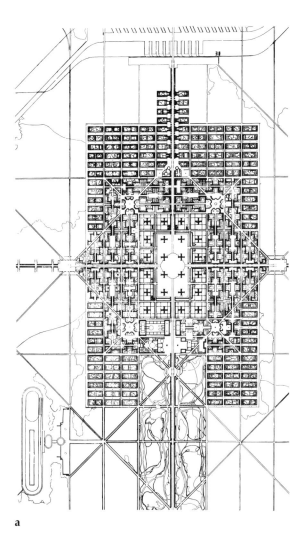

a

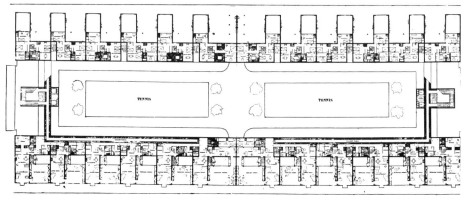

b

Immeuble Locatif in Stuttgart, and the Immeuble for Artists, another studio version, all of 1928. Finally, the Unité d'Habitation is really the practical culmination of the series. All of the elements of the prototype are here: the double-height living room, the two-level units, the hanging garden (now a balcony), the common services, and the building set in a dense urban setting with garden all around. The Unité in Marseille was the first Immeuble to be actually built, the realization of an idea born twenty-six years earlier.

a
Spangen Quarter, typical floor plans.
b
Spangen Quarter, site plan (left), gallery plan (right).

Spangen Quarter
ROTTERDAM, 1919–1921

Michiel Brinkman

Part of a district of low-income housing commissioned by the municipal housing authority, the Spangen Quarter includes the work of J. J. P. Oud, Jan Wils, and Michiel Brinkman, among others. The projects consist mostly of large, rectangular, four-story blocks that are typically bleak and anonymous on the street but open to garden spaces within. This rather private garden area is augmented in the neighborhood by parks and public spaces that open to the canals. The idea for the large block probably comes from Berlage and his plan for Amsterdam Zuid; it was his preferred prototypical building in his version of the garden city.

Brinkman's project consists of a rectangular block about 470 × 260 feet. It is four stories high, with an interior garden divided into two more or less equal courtyards that are further divided by wings projecting from the main block. The central transverse wing contains all common facilities such as the heating plant, laundry, washrooms, and children's play space on the terrace. A network of pedestrian walks and service streets for vendors connects all areas inside to a few gates and vertical service cores on each side of the block. Access is from the street to the interior garden and from there to each individual unit.

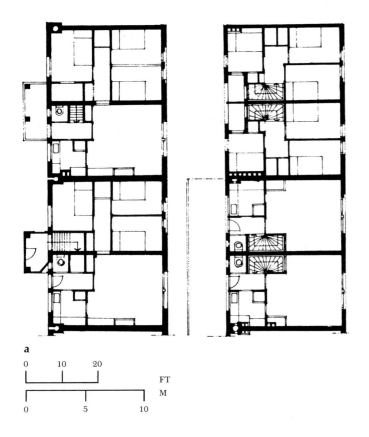

a

```
0    10    20
                FT
                M
0     5    10
```

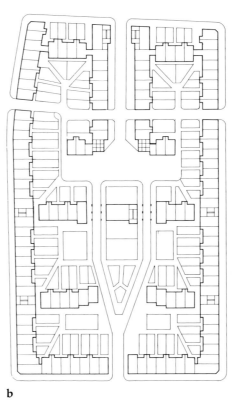
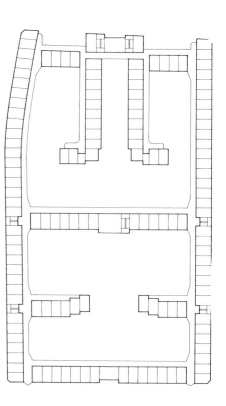

b

100

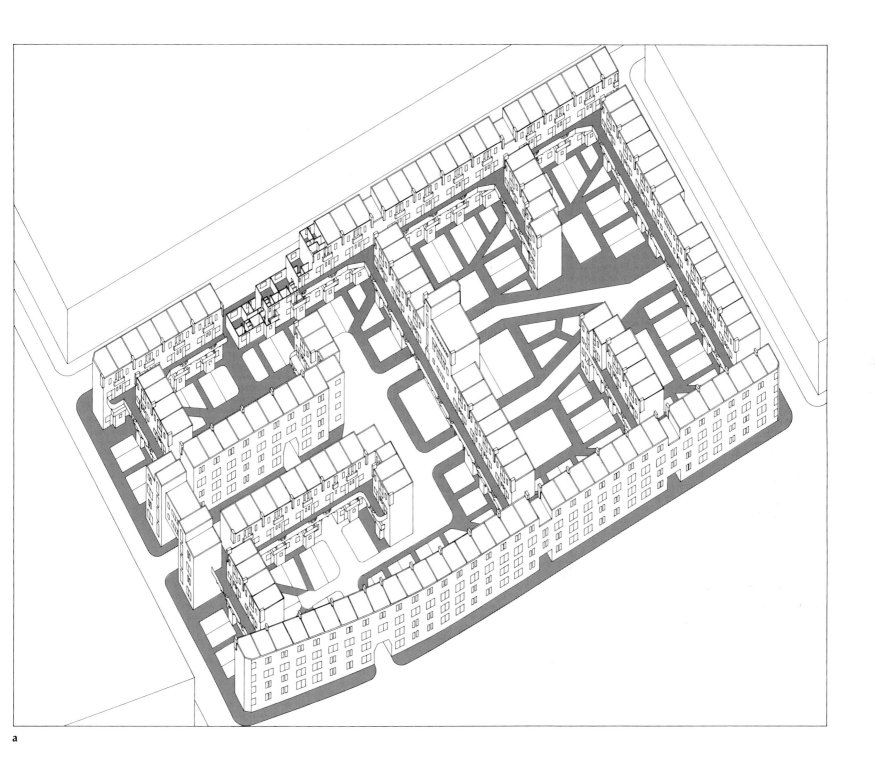

a

a
Spangen Quarter, garden facade.
b
Spangen Quarter, street facade.

a

b

a
Spangen Quarter, view of gallery.

In addition to access at ground level, there is an open, external gallery at the third floor that is connected to the ground by stair towers and elevators (for vendors' carts) located at each entrance to the block. This elevated street gives access to the upper units. The four-story blocks are divided into small three-bedroom units on the first and second floors and three-bedroom duplexes above. Access to the first two levels is directly from the garden and, to the second level, via independent stairs. The building is plain, mostly wall, on the street side. Inside, the surface is highly articulated with many windows and balconies. The concrete gallery, a detailed, freestanding structure in contrast to the continuous brick surface of the building proper, is of varying width and is provided with sitting areas and built-in planters.

Although stylistically similar to the surrounding buildings and basically reminiscent of the proto–art nouveau Amsterdam School, Brinkman's Spangen block is still a tour de force in its own right. The curse of the four-story walk-up apartment is virtually eliminated by the gallery and its elevator connection with the upper units. Because it is quite wide, the gallery is also a poor man's version of a terrace opening directly off the apartments; it may be used as a play space for small children, as a conversation area, for vendors, for bicycle storage, and so on. Spangen is especially significant because it seems to anticipate future trends. In particular, the gallery predates Ginzburg's street-in-the-sky in Moscow, Le Corbusier's Unités, and English projects of the fifties and sixties. Although not industrialized, Spangen also seems to foreshadow the advent of mobile, industrialized housing. Its basic idea would readily accommodate stacked modular, mobile units; a gallery, prefabricated like Brinkman's, could be added later to give access and fire exit to the units on top.

a

a
Nirwana apartments, site plan.
b
Nirwana apartments, typical floor plan.

Nirwana Apartments
DEN HAAG, 1927–1930

Johannes Duiker

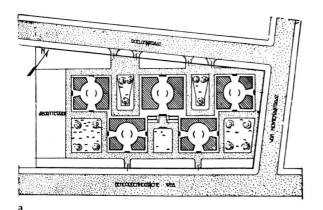

a

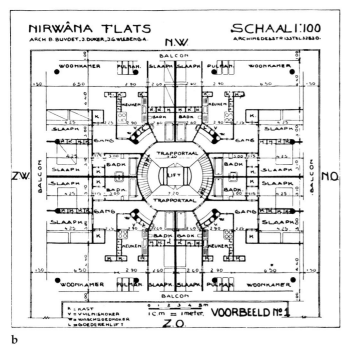

b

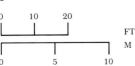

Like projects by many Dutch architects of the first two decades of the century, the early work of Duiker and his sometime partner Bernard Bijvoet was a mixture of Berlagian and Amsterdam School notions, a rather literal reinterpretation of the *Wendingen* publication of early Frank Lloyd Wright projects and the elementarism of De Stijl. The house that Duiker and Bijvoet designed at Aalsmeer in 1924 is the culminating work of this period, incorporating a little bit of all these attitudes.

After the design of the Diemerburg laundry in 1924—a simple, straightforward concrete and glass building—and the Zonnestraal tuberculosis sanitorium of 1926–1928, a definite functionalistic attitude emerged: a preference for industrial glazing, exposed structure, and irregular plans. Zonnestraal became the canonical building of the "Nieuwe Zakelijkheid" (the New Functionalism group in Holland apparently under the influence of Russian constructivism as exported via El Lissitsky, who was visiting in Holland from 1922 to 1926) and set the pattern that Duiker and Bijvoet's work would follow until Duiker's death in 1935.

Although only one building was built in the Nirwana project, Duiker's original conception was for a checkerboard system of large blocks connected together with external balconies. Beginning as an idea for apartments serviced from a central kitchen, Duiker's proposed layout included five blocks. The typical floor plan in each block consisted of a central stair and elevator serving four apartments, one in each corner. Each apartment had a service elevator to the kitchen below. Apparently the service apartment idea did not prove feasible and was replaced with a cooperative apartment arrangement. Now with independent kitchens, the apartments ranged in size from large (1,150 square feet) two-bedroom, two-bath units with maid's room, to huge (2,500 square feet) three-bedroom, two-bath units with maid's room. Enormous by Dutch standards, this scheme was later altered to provide between four and eight units per floor.

The original plan called for a concrete frame building with continuous cantilevered balconies; in the built version balconies cantilever at some corners but are integral with the building along each side. (The exterior walls, apparently made of concrete with interior cork insulation, leaked, and recent restorations have been undertaken to alleviate this problem.) The frame of the built version is clearly expressed by clerestory and larger operating windows that extend almost entirely along each side, stepping down to doors that open to the balconies. The build-up of glass detail toward the corner, along with the diagonal windows on some corners and the cantilevered balconies on others, emphasize the diagonal or "corner-on" view reminiscent of earlier De Stijl buildings. The corner becomes more of an obsession in later Duiker and Bijvoet work; in the Open Air School in Amsterdam of 1929 the entire building is rotated forty-five degrees to the street, the corner is now a two-way cantilever, and entrance is into the corner.

Nirwana apartments, axonometric.

a

Nirwana apartments, general view.

A curious six-story building rather outside the usual repertoire of modern housing—towers, slabs, rowhouses, and so on—and in its single-building version hardly inspiring the blessed condition the name might imply, Nirwana would still seem to offer a viable alternative for high-density housing. In the original version where there were several buildings, a very compact group resulted. Even though each building was separate, the connecting balconies would have given the impression of a continuous building but one open on all sides for maximum light and air.

a

a
Summer house, plan. Alvar Aalto, Muuratsalo, 1953.
b
City Hall, plan. Alvar Aalto, Saynatsalo, 1950.

Hansaviertel Apartments

BERLIN, 1955–1957

Alvar Aalto

Alvar Aalto was one of the architects invited to design an experimental building for the Interbau Exhibition in the bombed-out Hansa district of Berlin. Like most of the projects there, the Aalto block is a freestanding building surrounded by open space and formally unrelated to neighboring housing projects. These apartments incorporate organizational themes that are long-standing in the Aalto oeuvre: the atrium house and the roman forum. Aalto's reference to these two spatial prototypes is continuous for over forty years, and most of his buildings in some way focus upon a courtyard or central void.

The courtyard may take the form of an enclosed, private outdoor space, as in the Villa Mairea of 1938, where the garden and pool area is defined by the house on two sides and a stone wall on the other, as in Aalto's summer house at Muuratsalo, where a fanned group of structures describes a series of courtyards and the main house itself is a courtyard building, or the City Hall at Saynatsalo of 1950, where the building is wrapped around a raised, central garden. On the other hand, the courtyard may take the form of a large outdoor public space like a forum, semienclosed by large buildings, as in the Sanitarium at Pamio of 1938, where the courtyard space is also the entrance to the building, or the University of Jyvaskyla of 1952, where the buildings of the campus are built on three sides of an existing track. But the courtyard is not limited to external spaces, and central, usually skylit voids occur as interior courtyards in many Aalto buildings, notably the Finnish Exhibition of the New York World's Fair of 1938, the lobby cafeteria of the Rautatalo office building in Helsinki of 1951, the skylit library and upper terrace of the Cultural Center at Wolfsburg of 1958, or the main sales area of the Academic Book Store in Helsinki of 1966.

The Hansaviertel block is not the exception to the rule, and two courtyard concepts are applied here. Entrance to the building from the street is through a partial courtyard formed by the projecting wings into a lobby that may also be interpreted as an atrium space. But more importantly, each apartment within is itself a miniature atrium house, containing a large paved, outdoor terrace onto which the living room, dining room, and master bedroom open.

One-, two-, and three-bedroom units as well as studios are available in each block, for an unusually wide range of unit types. Kitchen and bathroom services are backed up to adjoining walls and corridor walls, freeing all exterior surface for bedroom windows. A separate lobby area with elevator and stairs serves each block.

Aalto's Hansaviertel block is a rather useful urban prototype. Although the Berlin building has open space on all sides and the building is planned so that windows are required on all sides, only slight modification could make it suitable for a continuous building type with preferred sides. The garden-apartment-in-the-sky or patio-house-in-the-sky is not a new idea—Le Corbusier

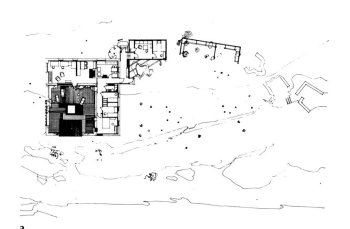

a

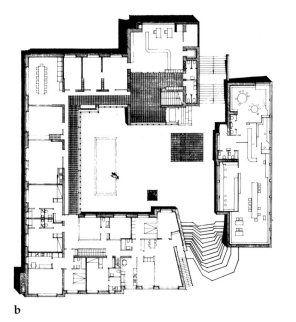

b

108

Hansaviertel apartments, axonometric.

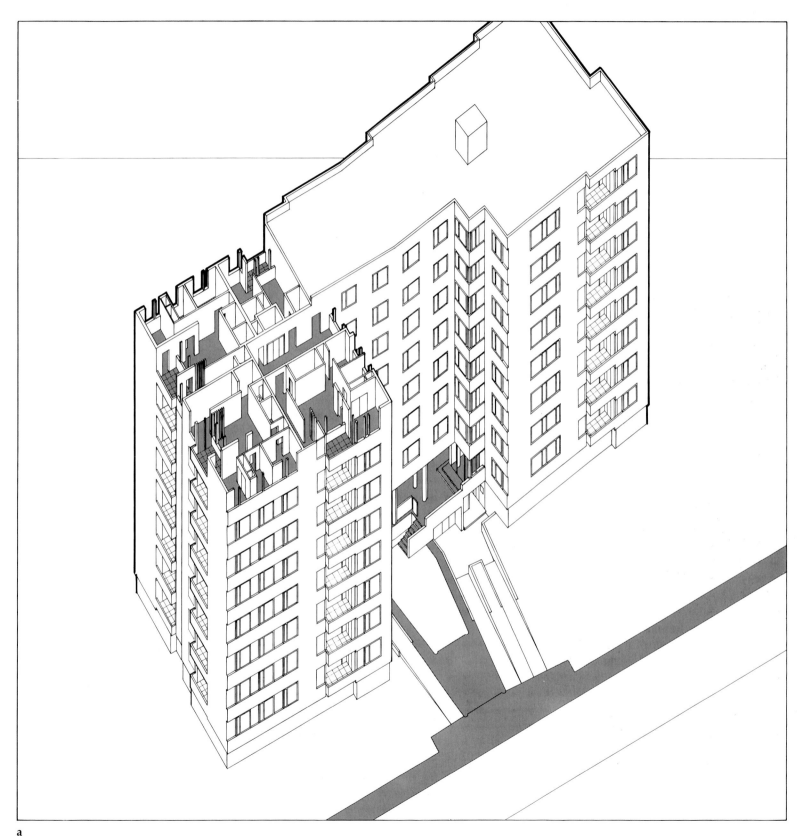

a

a
Sanitarium, site plan. Alvar Aalto, Pamio, 1938.
b
Rautatalo office building, plan. Alvar Aalto, Helsinki, 1951.
c
Hansaviertel apartments, ground floor plan.

was proposing a similar idea with his Immeuble Villas projects of the twenties —but unlike their predecessors, Aalto's units are well within the size restrictions of typical apartments (1,000 square feet here for a three-bedroom unit as compared to 4,000 square feet for Le Corbusier's Immeuble Villas units) and are a practical solution to a rather utopian concept.

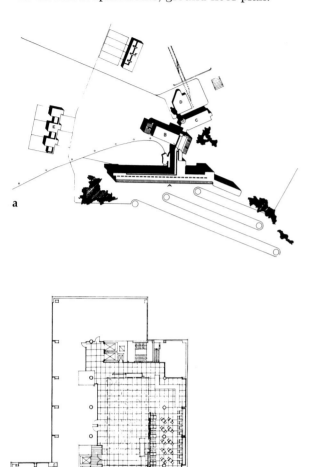

a

b

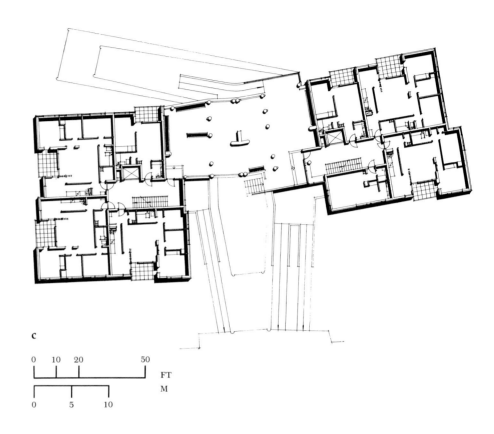

c

0	10	20		50	

FT

M

0		5		10	

111

Slabs

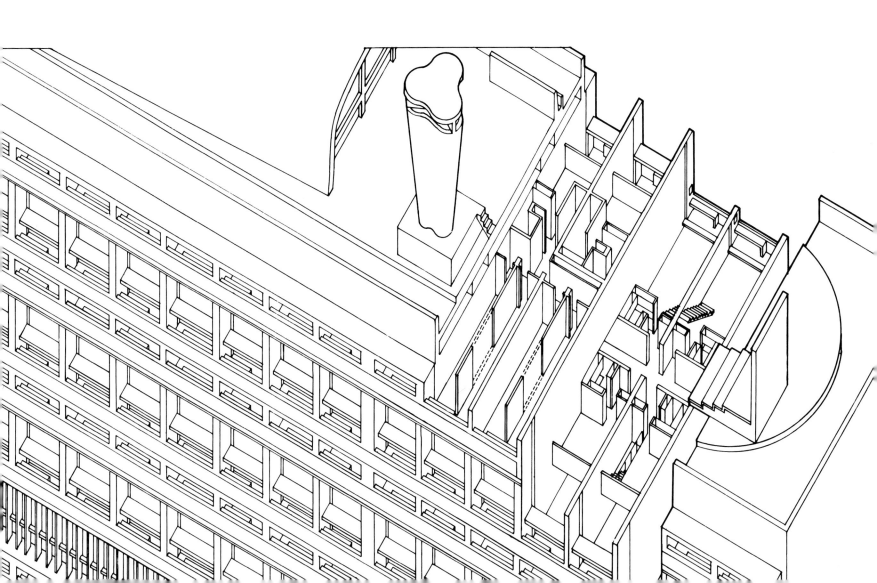

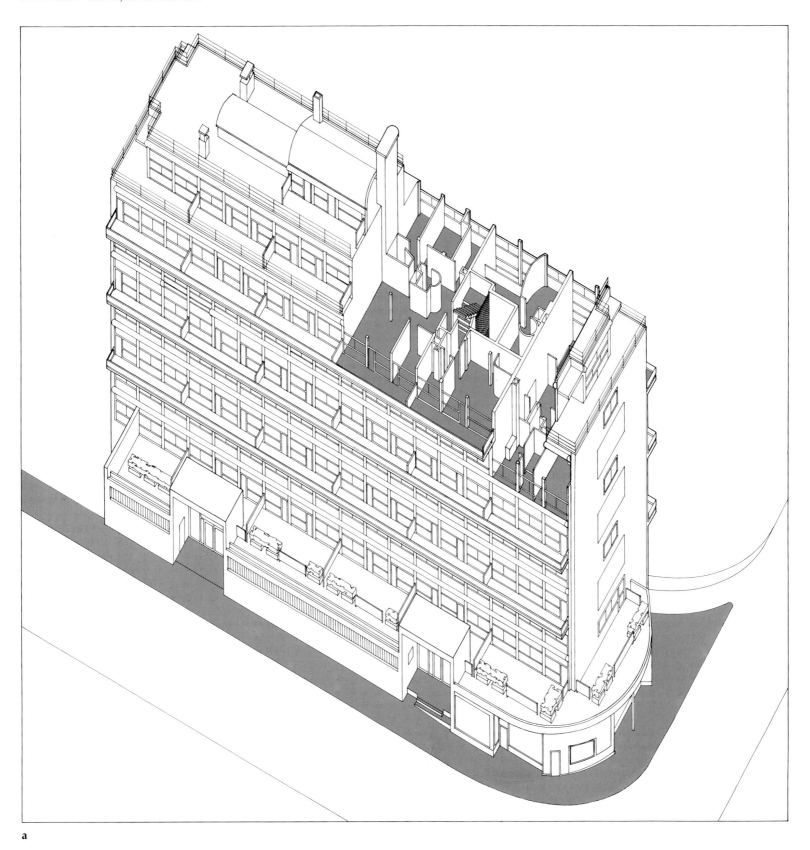

a
Immeuble Clarté, section.
b
Immeuble Clarté, typical upper-floor plan (left), ground-floor plan (right).

Immeuble Clarté
GENEVA, 1930–1932

Le Corbusier

The first of Le Corbusier's great apartment buildings to be actually built, Immeuble Clarté retained many of the virtues of the Immeuble Villas or multistory villas of the twenties, but in an economically more realistic package. The two-story units with double-height living rooms are taken from the earlier Immeubles, as are the hanging gardens, which at Clarté take the form of a continuous balcony rather than a volume within the framework of the building. Clarté was also to set the standard for later developments, particularly the Unité projects of the fifties and sixties. The extensive use of glass (locally the building was referred to as Maison de Verre), the attached brise-soleil (in this case a combination of roll-down awnings and balconies), the public rooftop terraces, the differentiated base upon which the building sets, and the exaggerated entrance all are ideas that were later incorporated into the building

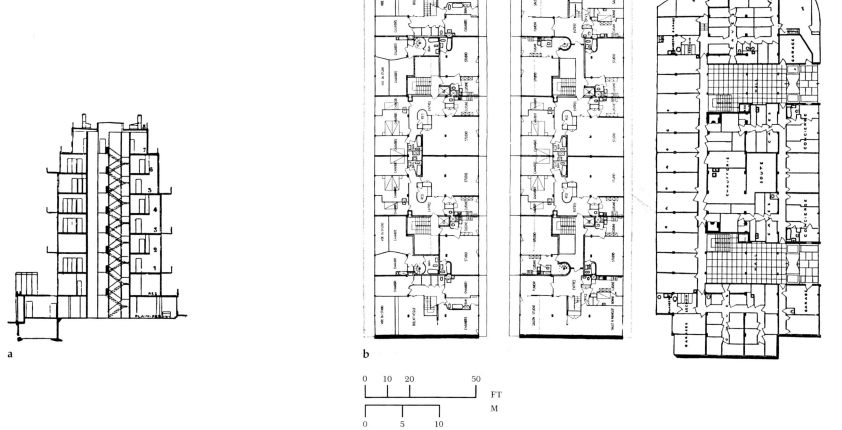

a

b

0	10	20		50	
					FT
					M
0		5	10		

115

Immeuble Clarté, entrance facade.

a

repertory of Le Corbusier. Clarté became an evolutionary piece leading toward the ultimate villa-in-the-sky, the Unité d'Habitation.

Situated on a difficult sloping site, Immeuble Clarté consists of a slab of apartments arranged around two stair and elevator cores set on a platform containing several shops, storage, caretaker's quarters, and garage space. The shape of the base is a function of the configuration of the site, while the dimensions of the slab are more a function of convenient apartment layout. Entrance to the vertical cores of the slab is through two large porticos that project up from the platform. The top of the platform serves as terrace space for the first level of apartments.

In many ways Clarté is similar to the Wanner project in Geneva of 1928–1929. There, balconies have replaced terraces and the double-loaded, skip-stop corridor has been replaced by the double core arrangement, but some apartments still have double-height living rooms, the roof terraces are public, the building steps back toward the top and has much the same general appearance and proportion as Clarté. There are a variety of apartment types in Clarté, including one- and two-story units as well as studios and two- and three-bedroom units. Each unit has continuous balcony frontage with the exception of a few studio units. The larger two-story units, located along the south side and at the ends, include a spacious library and dining room.

Immeuble Clarté is surely one of the great buildings of the period and one of Le Corbusier's important early projects. In recent years the building has been poorly maintained, but a group of local architects now own the building and are in the process of reconditioning it.

a
Narkomfin Apartments, unit plans.
b
Narkomfin Apartments, garden facade.

Narkomfin Apartments

MOSCOW, 1928

Moses Ginzburg and I. Milinis

By the mid-twenties in the Soviet Union it was clear that assigning each family to one room in a traditional apartment building with the bath and kitchen used collectively was not an acceptable housing technique and other methods would have to be developed. It was equally clear that there was no way to give every family a conventional apartment. In response to this problem the Association of Contemporary Architects (OSA) developed several proposals for communal houses aimed at providing collective facilities such as a canteen, kitchen, gymnasium, library, day nursery, and roof garden as justification for reducing the size of the individual unit. The Stroikom Units, as they were called, are some of the most interesting and innovative projects of the twenties and are certainly precursors of much European housing.

a

```
0    10    20         50
|----|----|----------|    FT
                          M
|------|------|
0      5      10
```

b

Narkomfin Apartments, axonometric.

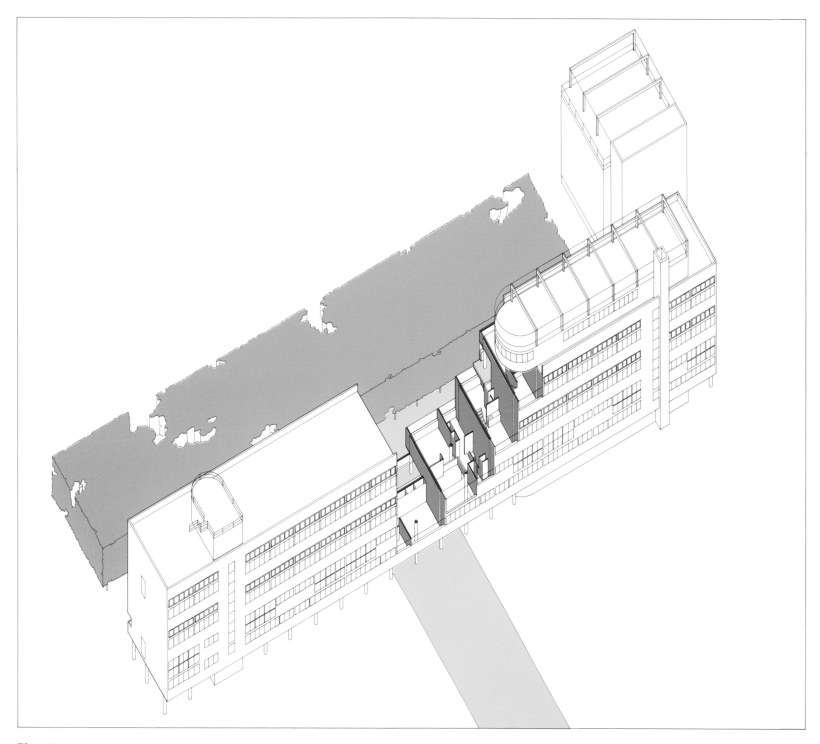

Plate 5

a
Narkomfin Apartments, plans, section, and elevation.
b
Narkomfin Apartments, perspective.

Narkomfin was an adaptation of two of the OSA units, both of which were two-level, through apartments reached by a single-loaded corridor at every third floor. Stairs led up and down from this wide so-called "interior street." The single-loaded corridor was thought to be preferable to a double-loaded arrangement because of the natural light along one side. One unit is a one-bedroom, two-room apartment and the other a two-bedroom, three-room unit. Both have double-height living rooms and minimum kitchen and bath facilities. The apartments are arranged in a slab raised off the ground. The top and ground floors are used for public services. Attached to the slab by the lower corridor is a block containing other collective functions.

Although never very popular because of their small size, the Narkomfin Apartments were an ingenious solution to a housing crisis and are still acceptable as studio units. Narkomfin is interesting also because it incorporates several ideas that were later modified and adopted by Le Corbusier: the building on pilotis, rooftop public or collective functions, skip-stop corridors, and two-level, through apartments. Later variations of the Narkomfin idea brought the corridor to the interior in a double-loaded arrangement, which, although much smaller, is exactly like the later, now-famous Unité section.

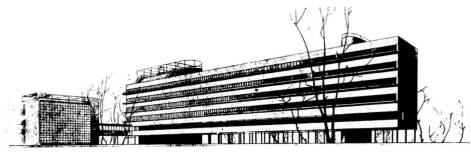

b

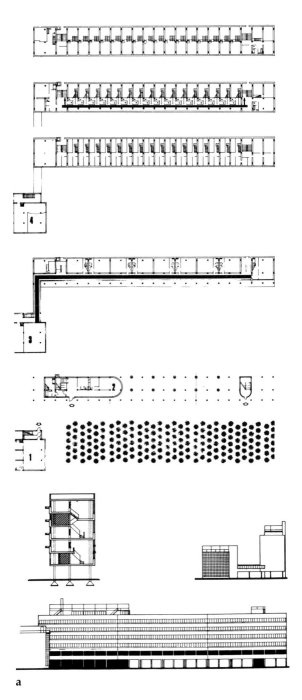

a

119

a
Unité d'Habitation, site plan.
b
Unité d'Habitation, section and elevation.

Unité d'Habitation

MARSEILLES, 1945–1952

Le Corbusier

In the twenty-three years between the first Immeuble Villas project of 1922 and the beginning of the Unité d'Habitation in 1945, Le Corbusier designed over thirty housing developments. Only a few of these were actually built, and aside from the ill-fated Bordeaux-Pessac project of 1923 and Le Corbusier's own apartment house, the Marseilles block was the first of the important projects to be built in France. It is the culmination of three decades of continuous development, really the first physical manifestation of all of Le Corbusier's ideas about the individual family unit, the grouping of units, and the city itself.

Le Corbusier repeatedly refers to the influence that his 1907 visit to the Carthusian monastery on the Ema near Florence had on the development of the Unité. Stemming from observations about the monastery—how individual units are arranged and then collected together—the Unité evolved from the Immeuble projects of the twenties and still shares many of their essential characteristics. The large courtyard blocks or continuous buildings of the earlier period have given way to a seventeen-story slab set off the ground on pilotis. The slab may occur individually or in multiples but it is always nearly the same. The long sides face east and west, as do the through apartments. Special apartments are on the south side, and the north wall is blank. There is a roof garden, integral brise-soleil and balcony, elevator access from a lobby among the pilotis, and in the Marseilles block, two floors of shopping midway up the building. The well-known section develops from a circulation system of corridors every third floor: access is from the corridor into two-level, through apartments that are L-shaped in section and interlock around the corridor.

The monastery prototype and subsequent examples of the early Immeubles up to the buildings that appear in the Ville Radieuse in 1935 are single-loaded corridor versions of the skip-stop arrangement. There is speculation that the idea of the Unité section was copied from Moses Ginzburg in 1928, when Le Corbusier observed the construction of the Narkomfin apartment building in Moscow. Perhaps his ideas were reinforced by what he saw there, but the notion—spatially—had been around for some time. The section of Villa Carthage of 1928 only needs a central corridor to become the typical Unité section. Any of the double-height Immeuble types including Garche and Meyer are volumetrically very similar to the Unité section, or at least to half of it. The Immeuble Villas of 1922 were a single-loaded, skip-stop arrangement, and the Ginzburg section was, after all, based upon a single-loaded, skip-stop corridor, too. At any rate, the section was fully developed with Ville Radieuse and was only further refined with the typical unit plans of 1937 and the subsequent development of the brise-soleil.

After the Rio de Janeiro experience in 1936 and that of Algiers in 1938 Le Corbusier greatly increased his emphasis on sun control. The purpose of the brise-soleil is to let sun in during the winter and keep it out during the sum-

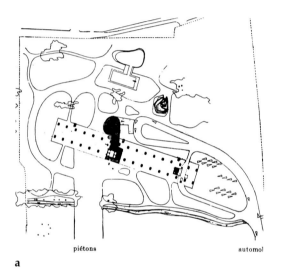

piétons   automol

a

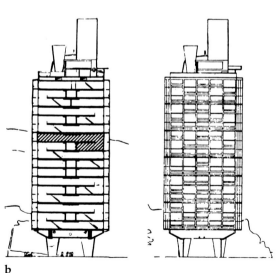

b

Unité d'Habitation, axonometric.

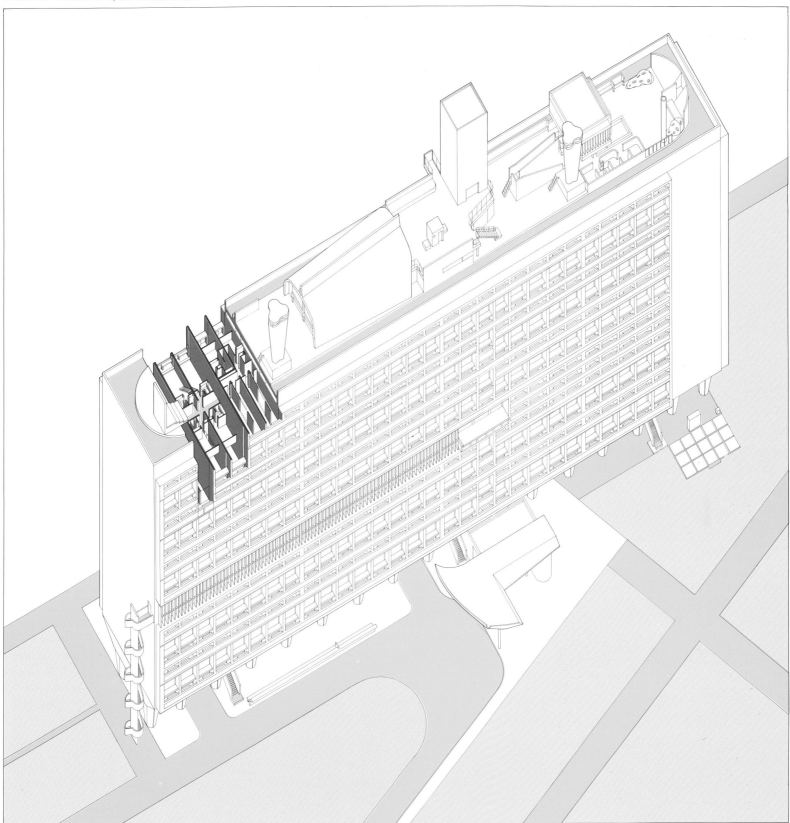

Plate 6

Unité d'Habitation, facade.

a

a

Unité d'Habitation, detail.

a

123

a

a
Unité d'Habitation, unit section and plans.
b
Unité d'Habitation, entrance.

mer. In his dialogue about sun control Le Corbusier dates the development of the brise-soleil with Villa Carthage of 1938, but the brise-soleil as it came to be widely used becomes an integral part of the facade in the Algerian projects. The standard orientation of a Unité is also a function of the movement of the sun: the building is situated so that each apartment gets sunlight sometime during the day.

Le Corbusier designed several variations of the Unité: Nantes-Rezé, Briey-en-Forêt, Berlin, Meaux (not built), and the most recent, Firminy, which was finished in 1968. Subsequent versions of the Marseilles block have suffered from more stringent economic restrictions. The double-height living room at Marseilles is drastically reduced at Nantes-Rezé and disappears altogether at Firminy, with depressing consequences to the already small space. The articulation at mid-building afforded by the two-story zone of commercial and office space at Marseilles was not possible in later programs, and the results are plastically less satisfying. The roofscape, so dear and ideologically essential at Marseilles, is but the ghost of its former self at Briey-en-Forêt, and Firminy has been so cheapened and stripped of excellent detail as to seem to be almost of another hand.

The Unité was not without its problems, and perhaps Lewis Mumford's disapproval of "a monument brilliantly disguised as a housing project" was partly deserved. The apartments are too narrow, the hallways long and dark, the space under the pilotis not very usable, and of course the supermarket did not work (although that space now is mostly used as architects' offices) and, as it turned out, was not really for poor people. Still, the Marseilles block is probably the most copied building of the twentieth century. Its influence on the form of subsequent housing has been profound, and variations of it can be seen in almost every country, built under widely varying conditions. It may be a monument disguised as housing, but modern housing and the Unité d'Habitation are synonymous.

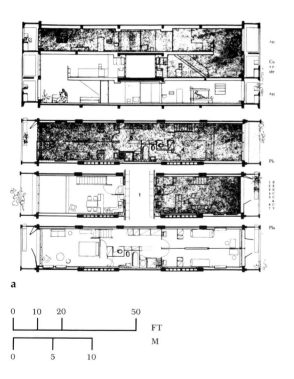

a

```
0    10   20           50
├─┼─┼─┼──────────┤
                     FT
                     M
├────┼─────┤
0    5     10
```

b

125

Harumi Apartment House

TOKYO, 1958

Kunio Maekawa

High-rise buildings until very recently were an anomaly in Tokyo; the Harumi slab is one of the exceptions. It is clear from the massive concrete structure that earthquake loading was a foremost consideration in this ten-story elevator building. Begun in 1956, the Harumi Apartment House was the first high-rise elevator building to be sponsored by the Japanese Housing Corporation.

There can be no doubt that contemporary Japanese architecture has been greatly influenced by the later work of Le Corbusier. Maekawa, in fact, spent two years in Le Corbusier's rue de Sevres atelier, from 1928 to 1930. It is not surprising, therefore, that the Harumi slab, although programmatically different from Le Corbusier's Unité at Marseilles built ten years before, shares many features of the Unité and might be thought of as its Eastern equivalent. Similarities include skip-stop corridor arrangements and integral balconies that

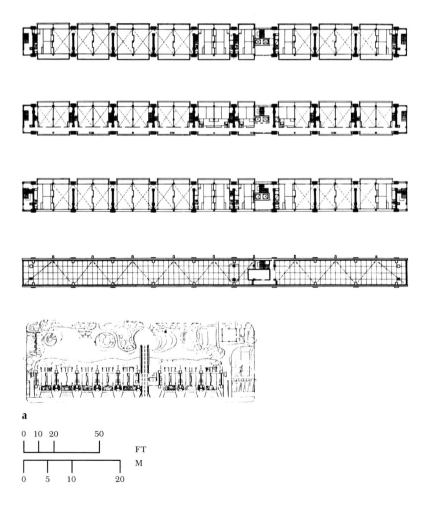

a

```
0   10  20        50
|   |   |         |
|   |   |         |          FT

                             M
|   |   |         |
0   5   10        20
```

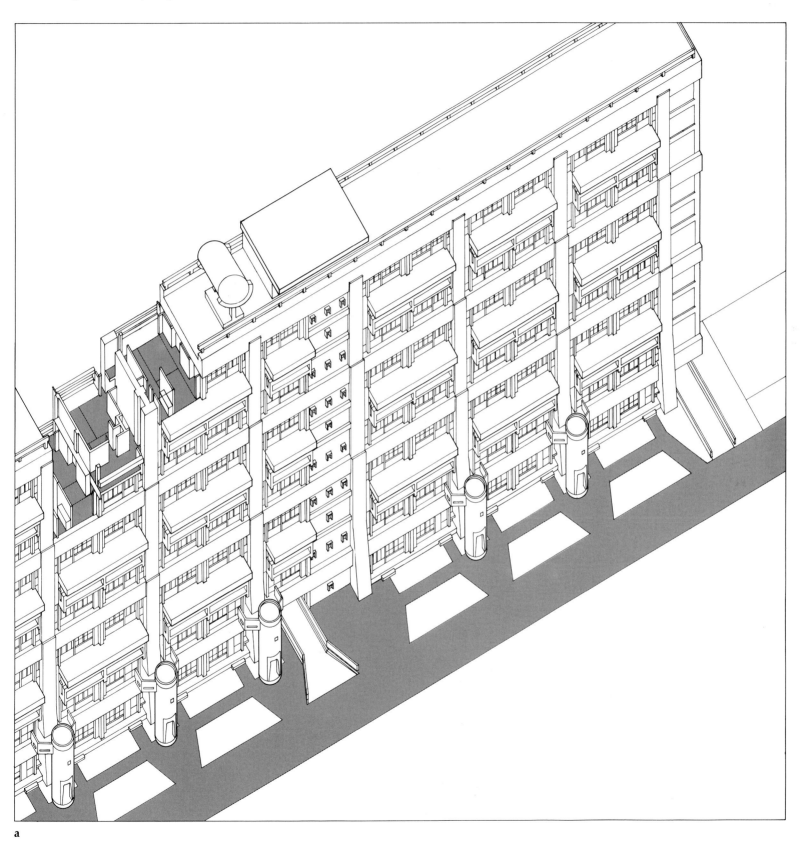

Harumi Apartment House, facade.

a

also serve as brise-soleil. Although the building does not rest on piloti, its juxtaposition with the ground plane is distinguished by a zone of unique apartments, the lobby, and on one side freestanding stairs that give access to the second level. The rooftop, like that of the Unité, is different from the repetitive elements of the elevation and terminates the vertical attenuation of the facade with a distinct horizontal lid; it is not intended for use by the occupants, however.

The apartments, although designed for an upper-middle-income market, are very small and consist of one Western and two Eastern style rooms. Access from the single-loaded, skip-stop corridor is via stairs up and down from the corridor to similar apartments at each level. Each apartment is arranged between a storage wall on one side and the shear wall with the service cores and stairs on the other. Although probably acceptable for the Japanese market, to the Western eye the apartments may be too small and lacking in variety.

The Unité prototype was intended as a freestanding building set off the ground to allow the groundplane to pass freely beneath and around it. This idea has obvious limitations in an urban setting, and Harumi does not rest on piloti. Set in a rather dense and random site, Harumi has the capability, by virtue of its size, concatenated nature, and its properties as a wall, to organize the buildings and spaces around it. Rather than a building in a space like the Unité, it is a building that defines a space and is therefore very adaptable as a dense, urban version of the Unité.

Durand Apartment Project
ALGIERS, 1933–1934

Le Corbusier

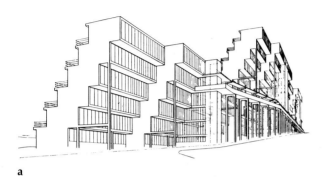

a

b

Combining the privacy of low-density terrace housing with the advantages of high-rise building, the idea of the stepped-section slab inevitably captivated architects preoccupied with inner city building. Probably no housing type has caught their fancy more, and countless versions of it can be found in almost any country under a variety of conditions, both as projects and as built examples.

It is impossible to establish the exact evolution of the stepped slab; reference to ancient examples such as the hanging gardens of Babylon or to any hillside terrace situation can be made. However, development of the stepped slab is dependent upon rigid frame construction, and hence it is a distinctly modern invention. Similarly, it would be difficult to demonstrate exactly where Le Corbusier got the idea for the stepped slab that appears in the Durand project of 1933. It may have been derived from the stepped-section building on the port development of Garnier's Cité Industrielle of 1904 or perhaps from Breuer's stepped-slab hospital of 1928. The idea may simply have come from the fusion of a Corbusian obsession with mass production and the paraphernalia of industrialization—particularly metal file cabinets and steamship trunks (preferably shown with drawers open)—and a fascination with gardens-in-the-sky as demonstrated in the Immeuble projects of 1922.

Durand may be thought of essentially as the typical Immeuble section—two-story units with large terrace and double-height interior void—but with units slipped past each other in section-like drawers, each unit opening to the terrace on the top of the unit below. Or Durand could be thought of as a precursor to the Unité d'Habitation: long narrow units two stories high, like rowhouses in the air, but again slipped past each other to allow terrace space, and corridor access every third floor.

The Durand units are large, ranging here from three-bedroom units of about 1,200 square feet, not including 300 square feet of terrace, to almost 3,000 square feet for a four-bedroom unit, not including 500 square feet of terrace. Each unit incorporates two-story spaces, and is certainly extravagant by today's standards; it is not surprising that the project, like the Immeuble Villas, was not built.

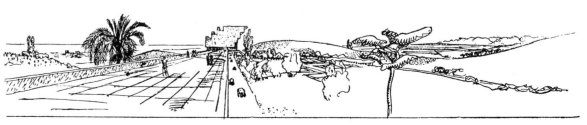

c

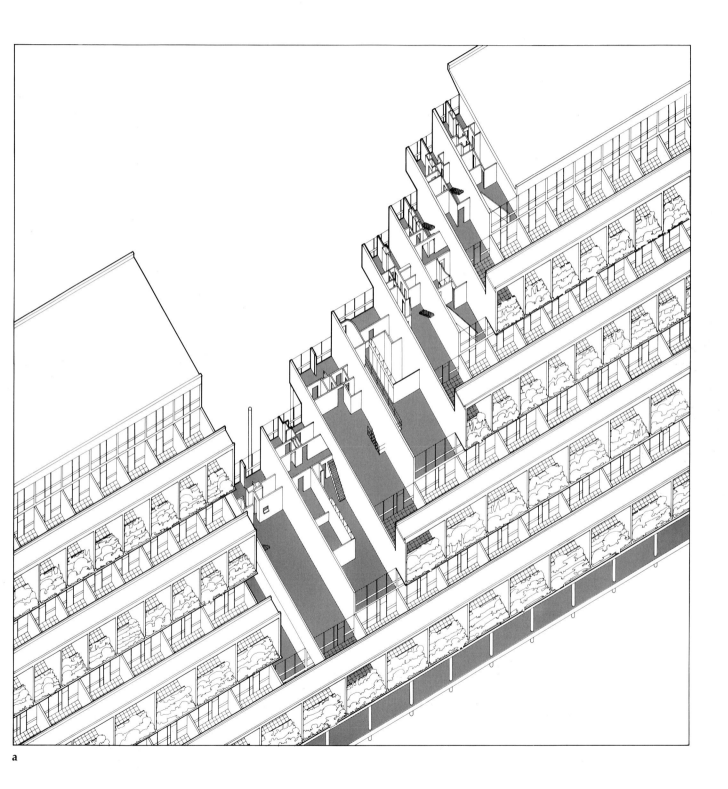

a
Durand apartments, section.
b
Apartments, section. Alison and Peter Smithson, project, 1952.
c
New Brunswick Center, perspective. Patrick Hodgkinson, London, 1958.

The stepped slab has some obvious limitations: units can be stepped back only so far before the building becomes structurally unstable. And although there is clear logic for stepping back to gain terrace space, the resulting space beneath the building on the opposite side is less logical. Durand is only four units high (eight floors) but sets on a three-story base of automobile circulation, parking, and a hotel. Unit size diminishes upward from this base, so that both undesirable conditions of the building type—structural instability and unusable space beneath the building void—are reduced. However, the three-story base seems to be an unlikely commitment to nonresidential space in a building of only eleven floors.

Stepping to the north, the terraces are equipped with continuous planters along the edge and covering pergolas. Together these elements create a foreground frame to a distant scene. The horizontal pergola redefines the implied two-story volume of unit and terrace and is the precedent for the famous brise-soleil that emerges in Le Corbusier's later apartment building of the same year, also in Algiers.

Although Durand had its problems, subsequent variations of it have even more problems. The Smithsons' proposal of the late fifties is twelve stories high with no service base. Horizontal circulation is on the terrace, an obvious contradiction to any notion of terrace privacy, which is further impaired at the ground floor because there is no separation between ground level and the first level of the bottom unit. The Smithson section is so narrow that a curving plan is required for lateral stability. If the typical units of Durand are huge, the Smithson units are ridiculously small, a kind of welfare state version of a grand idea even though the typical unit, like that at Durand, still has a double-height space.

Other attempts to mimic Durand, such as Hodgkinson's New Brunswick Center, a diminutive version of back-to-back Durands, have also not met with great success. The tremendous interior void between stepped slabs is essentially useless. Still, the idea remains attractive and probably viable. If energy shortages limit urban dispersion, it is likely that demand will increase for higher density forms of living that feature self-contained outdoor living spaces. The stepped slab is an obvious prototype for this kind of housing.

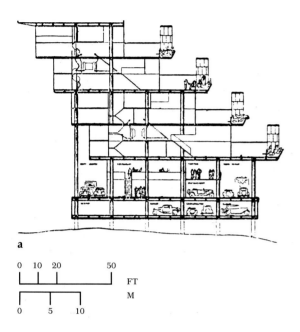

a

0 10 20   50
|__|__|_____| FT

                  M
|_____|_____|
0   5   10

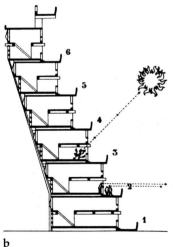

b

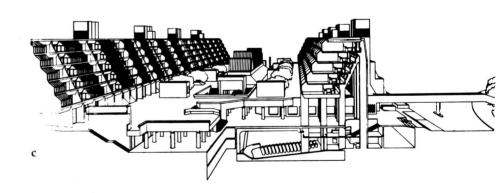

c

132

Zomerdijkstraat Atelier Apartments

AMSTERDAM, 1934

P. Zanstra, J. H. L. Giesen, and K. L. Sijmons

Apartment design is usually programmatically and functionally specific and consequently not very adaptable or easily changed. In this project for a block of apartments with studios, the strategy has been to provide a large studio space in each unit, with smaller spaces—the bedrooms, kitchen, and bath—as adjoining support areas. The central studio areas have high ceilings, and their large industrial-type windows face the street. The support functions, located in a zone on the opposite side of the building, have low ceilings and are on either one or two levels, depending on the size of the unit. The studio space can also be used as a multipurpose family living room.

There are several different split-level apartment types. The larger units have a kitchen, dining room, and small bedroom at the studio level and two bedrooms with bath above. Access to the upper level is by a small open stair on the support side of the studio. A variation of this is a one-bedroom unit with kitchen and dining area below and one bedroom with bath above. The small units have a kitchen, bath, dining, and sleeping space on a mezzanine that is connected to the studio level by a ladder. The three-bedroom units on the ground floor are somewhat larger than the typical three-bedroom unit because they are flush with the building line, while the main block of the slab sets back from the building line. Access is from repetitive stair and elevator cores in the support zone that serve two apartments per level.

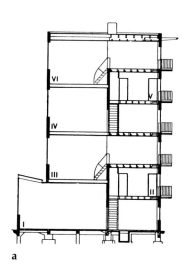

a

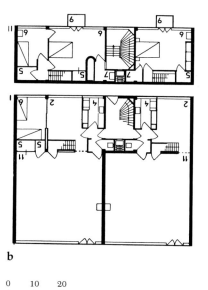

b

```
0    10   20
|—|—|—|          FT
                 M
0      5    10
```

c

133

a
Zomerdijkstraat atelier apartments, axonometric.

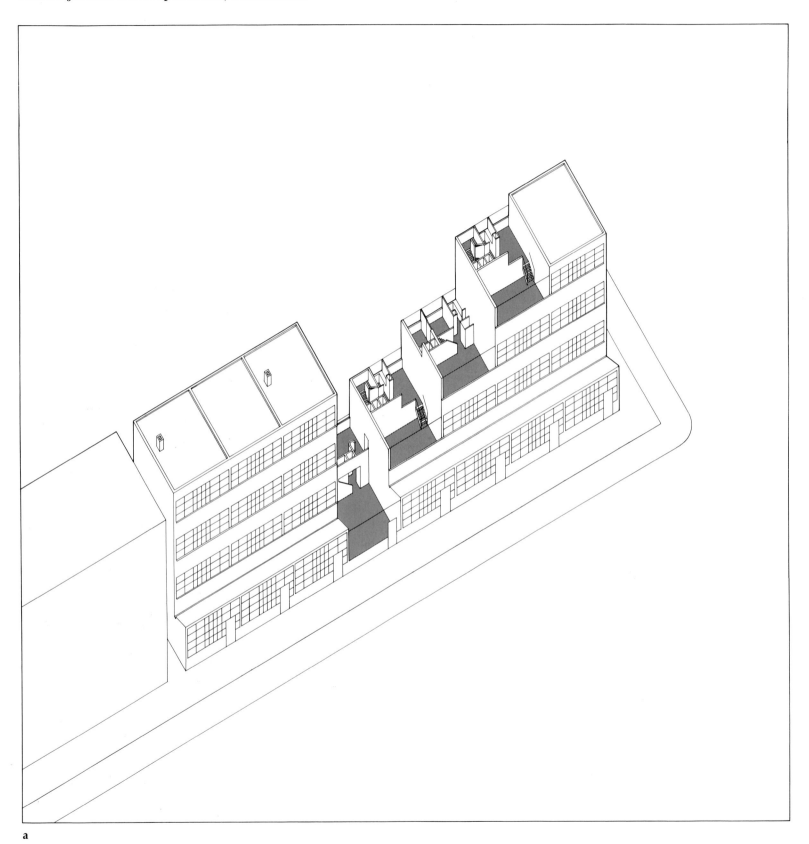

Zomerdijkstraat atelier apartments, street facade.

The building is simple and straightforward. The sectional idea of having large volumes on one half and the low-ceiling support on the other is consistently treated elevationally with a very flat surface and large areas of industrial sash on the studio side and small strip windows and balconies on the support side. Although the apartments are quite large and therefore probably not competitive economically, they are certainly attractive spatially and offer a high degree of potential user flexibility.

a

135

Towers

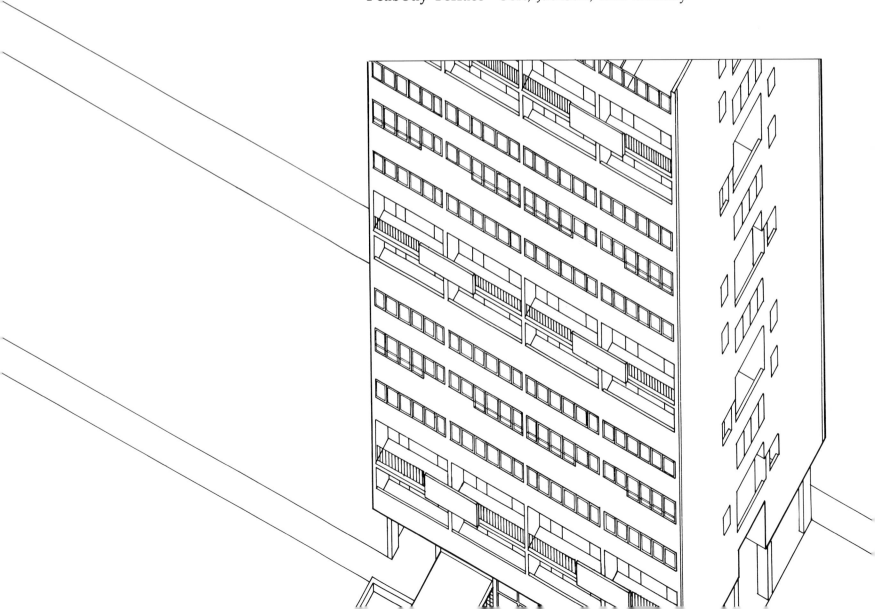

Victorieplein Tower, axonometric.

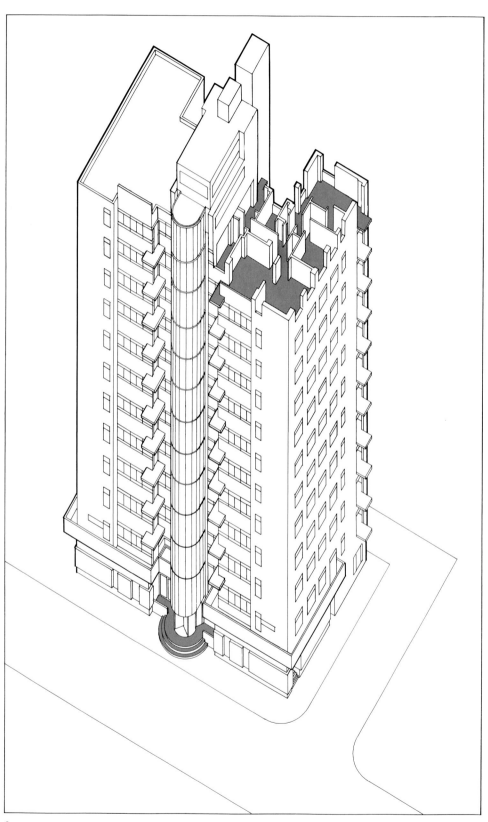

a

Victorieplein Tower
AMSTERDAM, 1929

J. F. Staal

Staal was a protégé of Berlage and earlier had been part of the so-called Amsterdam School. After about 1925 there was a general merging of *Wendingen*, De Stijl, and Functionalism, and Staal was one of the few personalities of the period who was able to capture and use the best ideas of each movement. Staal's work changes from a rather picturesque image of building—much under the influence of Berlage—around 1916–1925, to a much more doctrinaire, Functionalistic image by 1930. The Victorieplein Tower belongs to the later period and clearly is a composite of the formal ideas of the *Wendingen* group and the manipulations of detail and infatuations with jointure and the corner of De Stijl.

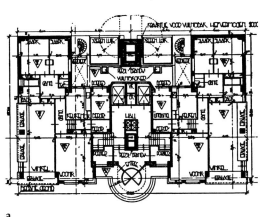

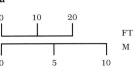

a

b

139

Aerial view of a portion of H. P. Berlage's "Amsterdam South" plan of 1915. The Victorieplein Tower occupies the axially dominant position in the lower right-hand corner.

a

a
Victorieplein Tower, garden facade.

Apartment towers of this period are unusual, particularly in Amsterdam, where soil conditions require pile foundations. Built on a Y-shaped site (the result of Berlage planning), the tower makes a strong statement about the use of the "point block" and stands out because it is much higher than the surrounding buildings and faces an open park space. It can be seen from some distance and dominates the surrounding space.

Victorieplein, which is thirteen stories high, is actually an H-shape in plan: two distinct parallel wings connected by a service core of stairs and elevators. The dominant stair on the entrance side is glass-enclosed and revealed to distinguish the entrance. Two different kinds of two-bedroom units are symmetrically arranged around the vertical core. Elements of Berlage theory may be seen in the symmetrical plans and in the axial properties of both the exterior glass-enclosed stair and the site, which was made to order for a tower. However, the influence of De Stijl and Functionalism has crept in with the extensive use of industrial glass on the front elevation for the main stair and balcony areas. Glass planes that turn the corner and balconies at the corner simultaneously emphasize and dissolve the corner—ideas reminiscent of De Stijl.

a

141

a
Hoogbouw towers, perspective.
b
Hoogbouw towers, floor plan.

Hoogbouw Towers
AMSTERDAM, 1927–1929

Johannes Duiker and J. G. Wiebenga

In 1930 Johannes Duiker and his partner at the time, J. G. Wiebenga, an engineer, published the book *Hoogbouw*. Literally "high-rise building," *Hoogbouw* was the published record of Duiker's ideas about housing. Along with setting municipal standards for housing, the book contained the design for a prototypical tower, including drawings of a typical group of towers. Duiker's ideas about housing are clear from articles that he wrote as editor of the magazine *de 8 en Opbouw* (see the November 1971 and January 1972 special issues of *Forum*). He found many advantages in high-rise building and considered this the ultimate move away from what he saw as the bourgeois attitude that each person should own his house and garden. High-rise building would free ground space for other activities and, in addition to the obvious building economies, would offer overall urban economies as well.

Hoogbouw, then, becomes the rather schematic product of Duiker's ideas about modern housing. Thirteen-story towers on an open site evidently constitute a typical arrangement. The typical tower contains four two-bedroom apartments back-to-back in two radiating wings, with four two-bedroom units back-to-back in the remaining opposite wings. The simple apartment plans consist of a hallway leading past the bedrooms to a living and dining space at the end that opens to a corner balcony. The wings with the two-bedroom apartments tend to form a wall running east and west to which the radiating wings

a

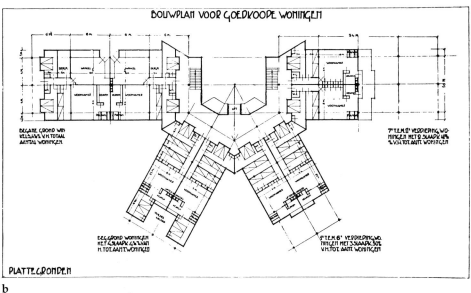

b

142

Hoogbouw towers, axonometric.

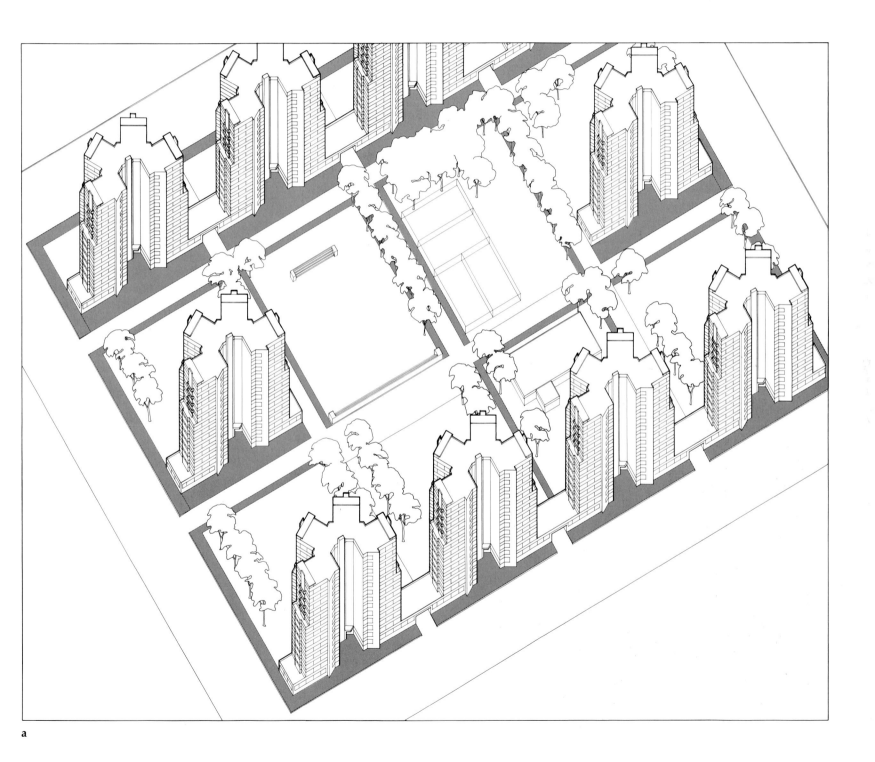

a
Hoogbouw towers, plans, elevation, and section.
b
Hoogbouw towers, site plan.

connect. All four wings in each building connect to a central curving elevator lobby. Each tower steps up from a base where two additional two-bedroom units on the bottom floors connect opposing east and west wings and begin to give the impression of a continuous, undulating building. Each lobby is entered from the curving courtyard and there is a breezeway between towers to the open space behind.

The rationale of the building plan seems clear: the radiating scheme lets light and air into each room. Similarly, there would seem to be clear logic for establishing the undulating wall: to give surface to the street. The logic of the site plan is less clear, however; if the wall orients the building toward the street with the radiating portion opening to the park, then there is an obvious contradiction where the radiating wings face the street on the opposite side of the group. Sun orientation may have been important with the radiating wings facing south, but still there are north-facing apartments, although they are kept to a minimum. The back-to-back apartment plans could easily be transformed to a double-loaded corridor slab on the wings that face the street; this is implied where the buildings connect together at the bottom floors.

It is conceivable that Hoogbouw simply represents the Dutch version of Le Corbusier's Plan Voisin of 1925: freestanding towers in a park-like landscape. In Plan Voisin, however, the towers were much taller (which Amsterdam soil conditions would probably disallow) and, significantly, they were office buildings and not housing, which was relegated to the lower Immeuble blocks. Hoogbouw combines the tower and the Immeuble, implying both high and low buildings. Amsterdam, of course, has been able to achieve high density without much high-rise construction, and nothing like Duiker's project has been built. The Dutch are more inclined to prefer lower, more compact living after the manner of Berlage's Mercatorplein housing of 1927 or the more recent projects by van Tijen and the van den Broek/Bakema partnership: low, dense buildings with both public and private spaces and a much smaller scale development.

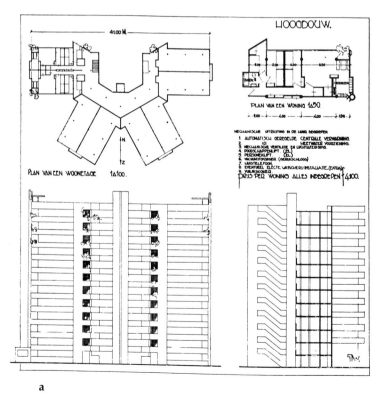

a

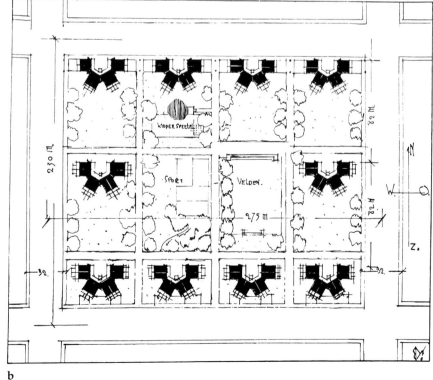

b

Price Tower

BARTLESVILLE, OKLAHOMA, 1953–1956

Frank Lloyd Wright

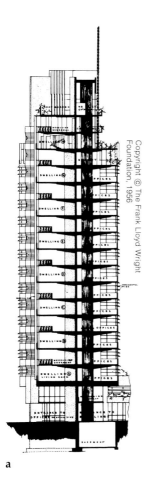

a

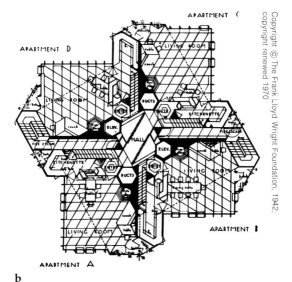

b

The Price Tower was the realization of an idea Wright had developed twenty-seven years earlier in New York City's St. Mark's Tower of 1929. It was not unusual for Wright to repeat a particular building idea: the use of cruciform plans in his earlier work is well known. Similarly, the California block houses and the Usonian houses of the twenties and thirties are recurring Wrightian themes.

While St. Mark's was a design for a freestanding tower, and the cantilevered, tree-like construction and the crossed-wall ideas were radically new, the superimposition of a diagonal organization (here a square rotated thirty degrees) was not. Wright had been experimenting with diagonal impositions for some time, beginning with the Lake Tahoe project of 1922 (where the cabin plans were a kind of superimposed grid), Taliesin at Spring Green of 1925, and San Marcos in the Desert of 1927, which uses a hexagonal system.

Experiments with towers or rotated square configurations and crossed-wall interior cores continued after St. Mark's Tower. The 1930 Grouped Apartment Towers for Chicago are really just St. Mark's repeated ten times in pairs and connected together, forming a continuous, undulating slab twenty-five stories high rather than the nineteen of St. Mark's. The tower appears again in Broadacre City of 1934; and in 1936 the Laboratory Tower at Johnson and Sons, although not made of rotated squares in plan, is still a version of the principle of cantilevering floors from a central core. Suntop Homes of 1939 is but an unrotated version: a typical two-floor apartment from St. Mark's adapted for family use and set upon the ground in suburban Philadelphia. It is all there: crossed-walls, two-story living room at the corner, balconies, and three floors because there were extra bedrooms in the program. And in 1940 yet another version of St. Mark's appears—this time in cluster form with towers of varying heights on a substantial platform—in the Crystal Heights Hotel project for Washington, D.C.

In between these larger projects Wright was applying some of the same principles in his houses. The superimposed diagonal arrangement can be seen in the Willey house (1934); the Hanna house, with its hexagonal system (1937); and Taliesin West (1938), which is a kind of expanded Willey plan with some buildings belonging to the diagonal system. The Herbert Johnson house of 1937 is nothing more than the core system of St. Mark's enlarged to such a scale that the spaces of the house are now incorporated within the core configuration and exterior space consists of the voids at the corners.

When St. Mark's was finally built in the form of the Price Tower at Bartlesville, the program had changed. The apartment building rising abruptly from the ground without adjacent ground-level structure was altered to provide a utility company office, a shop, the caretaker's apartment, covered parking, and considerable landscaping. The St. Mark's plan with a two-story apartment in each corner, was changed to meet office requirements: only one corner on

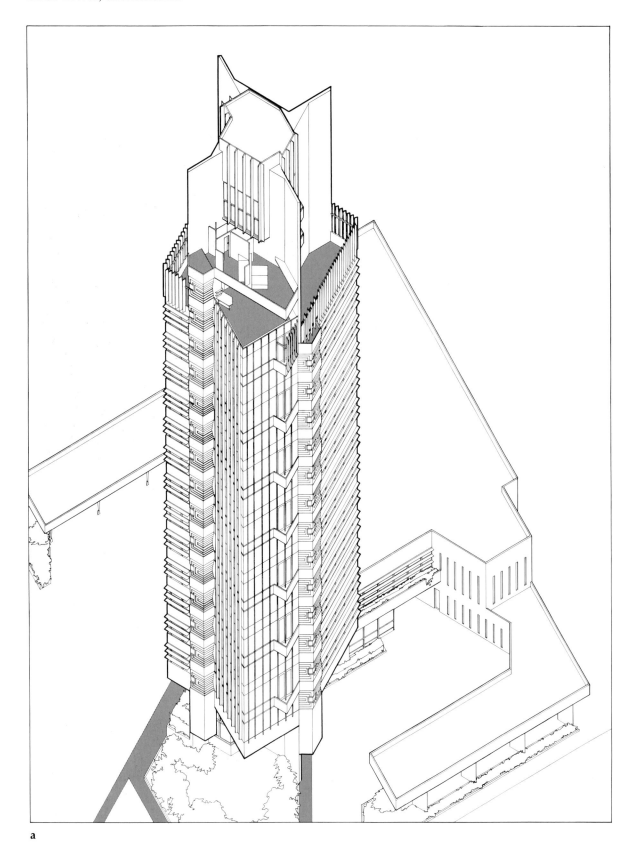

a

Price Tower, general view.

a

a
Grouped Apartment Towers, perspective. Frank Lloyd Wright, Chicago, 1930.
b
Hanna house, plan. Wright, Palo Alto, 1937.
c
Herbert F. Johnson house, plan. Wright, Wind Point, Wisconsin, 1937.
d
Price Tower, ground-floor plan.

each two floors was now apartment space and the rest was used for offices, with two separate lobbies below. The typical apartment remained unchanged: kitchen, dining, and living areas were at the entry level and upstairs, on the diagonal balcony overlooking the living room, were a large bedroom, a boudoir, which could double as a second bedroom, and a bath. The kitchen, bath, stairs, and fireplaces back up to the structural cross-wall, which contains all duct work, firestairs, and elevators.

There would doubtless have been some difficulties in marketing the apartments in St. Mark's: they were all the same size and were extravagant, with fireplaces on each floor, two-story spaces, large boudoir, and private elevator. So the addition of offices in the Price Tower is probably a sensible modification. The clumsiness of a slender tower meeting the ground is avoided in Price by the build-up of supporting spaces at ground level. The tower can be repeated to form a building like the Chicago apartments of 1930; this has the advantage of producing a mix of apartments and shows that the St. Mark's plan does not have to be freestanding. Whatever its faults, Price Tower is a remarkable building—structurally ingenious and architecturally rich—and it clearly demonstrates the great talent of Frank Lloyd Wright.

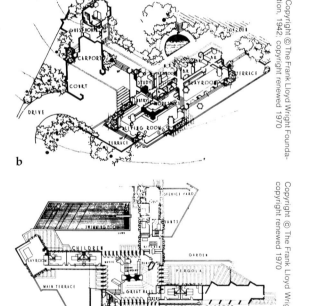

a

b

c

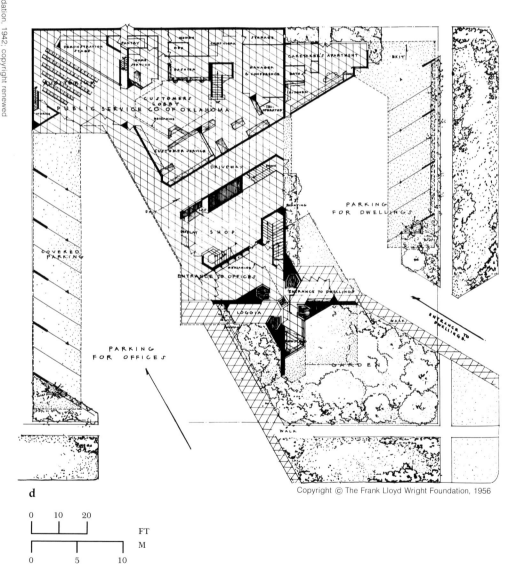

d

0 10 20
FT
M
0 5 10

Neue Vahr Apartments

BREMEN, 1958–1962

Alvar Aalto

The apparent result of a logical strategy—maximum good exposure—the twenty-two-story tower at Bremen may also be seen as an example of Aalto's continuing preoccupation with expanding radial or fan-shaped elements attached to regular solids. This form is applied to many different building types including, in addition to housing, public and institutional architecture. Examples of this persistent juxtaposition of fan-shaped and orthogonal systems include the Finnish Exposition at the New York World's Fair of 1938, a curving, stepped system of display panels inserted into a rectangular container; Baker Dormitories of 1947, a serpentine slab with regular, rectangular appendages; or the Pavia Housing Project of 1966, undulating slabs inserted into a regular grid system. The famous sketch of the project for the Göteborg City Hall of 1955—a regular system with a fan-shape attached that presumably responds to an irregular landscape—represents yet another variation. This formal strategy is repeated in many buildings, including the church at Imatra, a graduated, fan-shaped sanctuary attached to a regular vestibule and service block; the student hotel at Otaniemi; or any of the libraries, all fan-shaped reading rooms attached to a regular building of offices and support facilities. Bremen is just

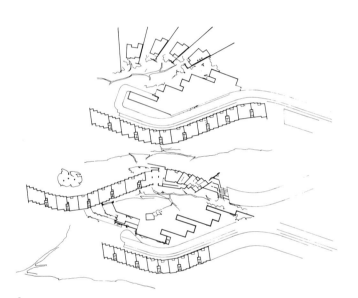

a

b

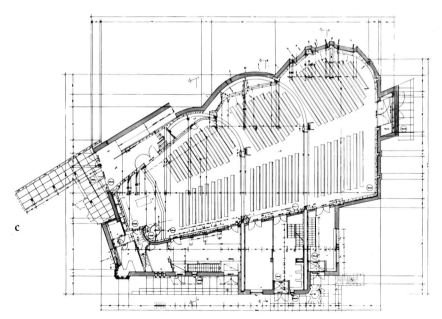

c

149

a
Neue Vahr Apartments, view from south.

a

a
Student hotel, plan. Alvar Aalto, Otaniemi, 1963.
b
Library, plan. Alvar Aalto, Seinajoki, 1963.
c
Neue Vahr Apartments, detail.

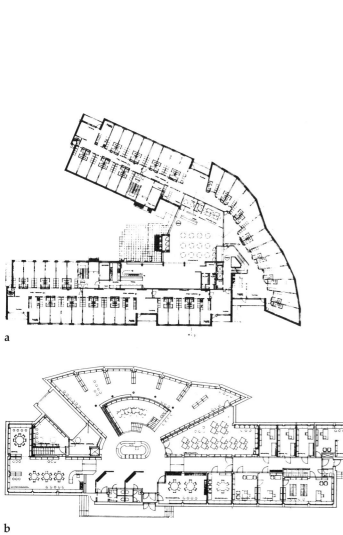

a

b

c

151

a

a
Neue Vahr Apartments, plan and sketch.
b
Neue Vahr Apartments, detail.

another variation of this idea; it might be thought of as a slightly modified version of the library plan extended vertically.

The fan-shaped plan of the Bremen tower presents a fresh approach to the design of single-loaded corridor apartment buildings. Following a formula that attempts to maximize preferred orientation and exposure and to minimize the service and access corridor, each apartment faces either south or west—an obvious advantage in a northern climate—and attaches to a service wall containing elevators and stairs. Kitchen and bath back up to this service wall; entrance is through this zone to the living and sleeping areas, which open to a large window and a modest balcony. Typical studio apartments are contained between a single-bedroom unit at one end of the corridor and a two-bedroom

0 10 20   50

FT

M

0   5   10   20

a

b

153

a
Neue Vahr Apartments, detail.
b
Neue Vahr Apartments, site plan.

unit at the other. An arcade lined with shops serviced from below connects the lobby of the tower with the adjacent shopping center. The fan-shaped side of the building opens to a park, and automobile parking at a lower level backs up to the service wall.

Although designed as a freestanding building in an open space, Bremen would seem to be more applicable as an urban building type. If the single-loaded corridor is extended, a serpentine, continuous type of building results. A single-loaded version of the Pavia slabs would be the logically consistent horizontal extension of the Neue Vahr Apartments. As compared to the freestanding tower, which needs open space all around, the continuous slab can connect buildings together, establish surface, adapt to various conditions, and help to complete existing urban fabric.

a

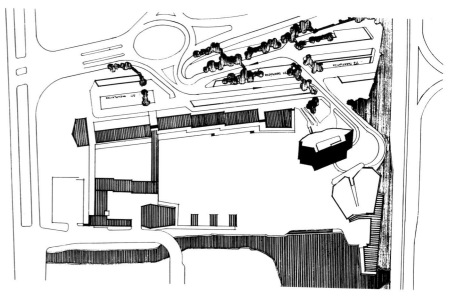

b

Hansaviertel Tower
BERLIN, 1960

J. H. van den Broek and J. B. Bakema

The van den Broek and Bakema tower of the Berlin International Building Exhibition of 1960 is probably the most important and innovative solution to high-rise, high-density housing to appear since Le Corbusier's first Unité d'Habitation of 1948 in Marseilles. Built as part of a rather picturesque scheme to rehouse about half of the six thousand residents of the bombed-out Hansa Quarter of Berlin, the van den Broek and Bakema building is one of six towers in a project that also includes six high-rise slabs and one- and two-story housing. The work of fifty-three different architects, including Gropius, Aalto, Neimeyer, and Le Corbusier, is represented.

The Hansaviertel tower shares many of the essential features of the Marseilles Unité: two-level, through apartments, balconies within the framework of the building, alternate corridors with apartment units above and below but with access from the corridor, partial detachment from the ground plane, and a rooftop intended for use by the occupants. This tower, however, probably offers a more realistic solution to the two-level, through-apartment, alternate-corridor arrangement. As satisfying as the double-height space in the Unité may be, its economic disadvantage is obvious. The stepped section in the Hansaviertel tower has a similar level change, but of only half a floor; and although there is no double-height space, there is some sense of spatial expansion along the hallway between the upper and lower levels. An additional advantage is

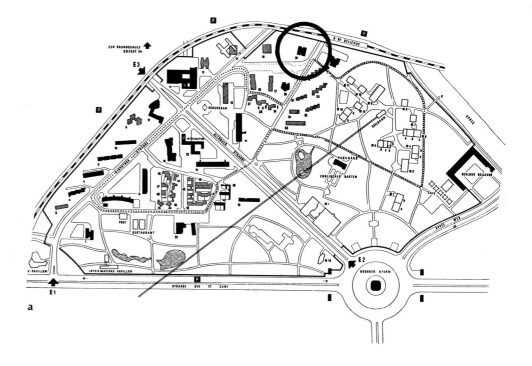

a

155

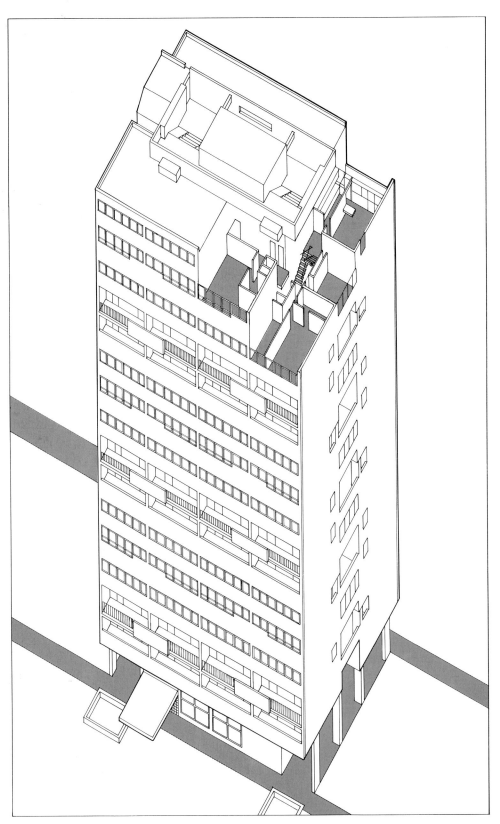

a

a
Hansaviertel tower, general view.

a

157

the 20-foot-wide bays as opposed to the 12-foot-wide bays in the Unité. This permits a variety of room sizes in a much smaller total area (860 square feet as compared to 1,200 square feet in the typical Unité apartment). The van den Broek and Bakema tower has another advantage over the Unité as an alternate-corridor arrangement: it is adaptable to United States fire codes, providing multiple exits from every level, even with the skip-stop configuration.

As built, the tower is only four bays wide because of the back-to-back arrangement of the stairs and hallways. More bays could be added, but this would require the addition of functionally unnecessary stair towers. The step-section and corridor scheme imply a slab-like or horizontal attenuation, but the building actually has more the appearance of a tower and is nearly square in plan. Finally, the section produces a specific mix of apartment types: four studio units are required on every fourth level, for an overall mix of fifty percent multiple-bedroom units and fifty percent studio units—certainly an unrealistic ratio for a normal housing situation and an inherent disadvantage of this section.

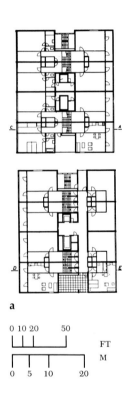

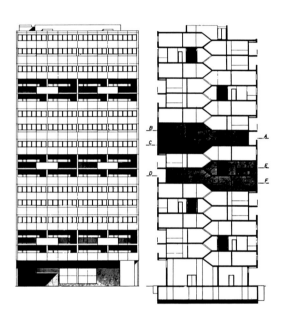

a

0 10 20   50
FT
M
0   5   10   20

158

Peabody Terrace
CAMBRIDGE, MASSACHUSETTS, 1964

Sert, Jackson, and Gourley

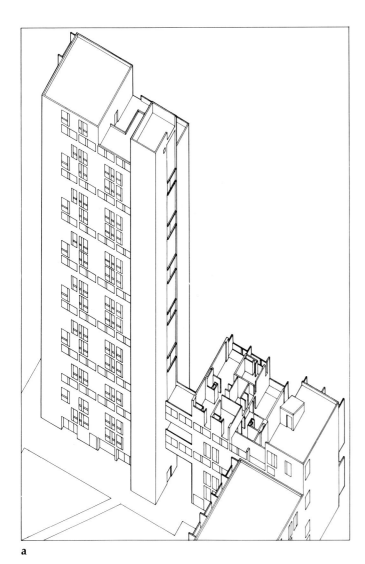

a

Only a short walk from Harvard Yard, this building complex on the banks of the Charles is another addition to J. L. Sert's set of towers that punctuate the skyline along the river. Built as a kind of stylistic appendage to the Holyoke Center of Harvard University which Sert designed earlier, these married students' apartments have access to Harvard Yard through a pedestrian network that stretches from the river through the arcade of Holyoke Center.

Three towers of twenty-two stories each connect to eight-story wings arranged to form small quadrangles. The quadrangles follow the existing pattern of housing along the Charles. Larger spaces to the perimeter contain recreational spaces, and a parking structure provides off-street parking. One of the rare examples of skip-stop planning in the United States, the towers are especially interesting as an innovative solution to the problem of how to take advantage of alternate-level corridors, meet national fire codes, and still produce an interesting building. The balconies solve the fire code problem by providing alternative exits via adjacent apartments. They also provide an outside living area and give sun protection to exposed sides. The balcony structure is laid over the surface of the building like a three-dimensional grid. This grid or matrix is contrived so as to be interesting and organizationally reflective of the every-third-level corridor system. There are several unit types. At the corridor levels where through apartments are not possible, there are small studio units with kitchen and living and dining areas, and one-bedroom units with living area and bedrooms to the outside opening to balconies. Noncorridor floors have one- and two-bedroom through apartments, always with the balcony to provide emergency fire exits. All apartments are arranged with services in one wall so that the opposite wall is uninterrupted from one end of the apartment to the other. This has the effect of spatially expanding the units, which are in fact quite small.

Although the balcony arrangement was an imaginative way to make a skip-stop package conform to fire codes existing at the time and simultaneously achieve a certain variety in elevation, there is some doubt that the skip-stop scheme is very advantageous. The alternate-level arrangement is perhaps more appropriate to two-level apartments, so that the stairs can be rather incidental and within the unit. Here, the stairs up and down from the corridors are enclosed fire stairs. However, the ingenious use of repetitive components including the balcony matrix and the window system has resulted in a building of considerable architectural interest.

Peabody Terrace, axonometric.

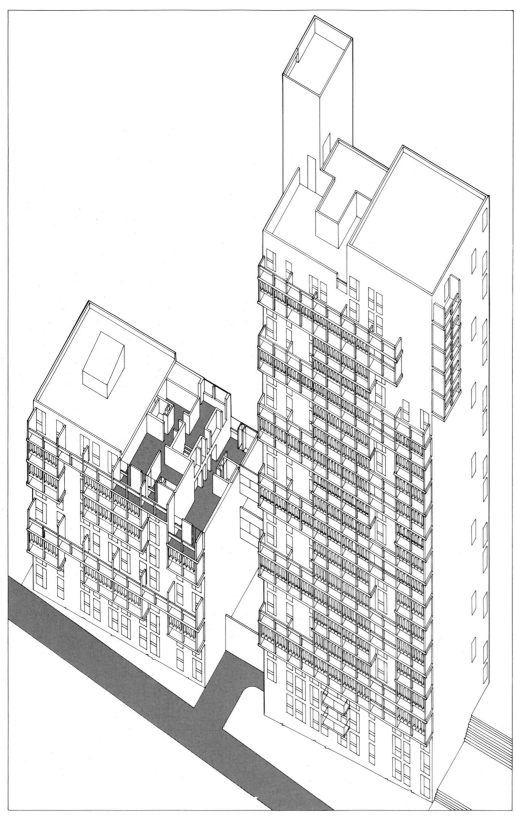

Peabody Terrace, aerial view.

a
Peabody Terrace, typical floor plans (left), site plan (right).

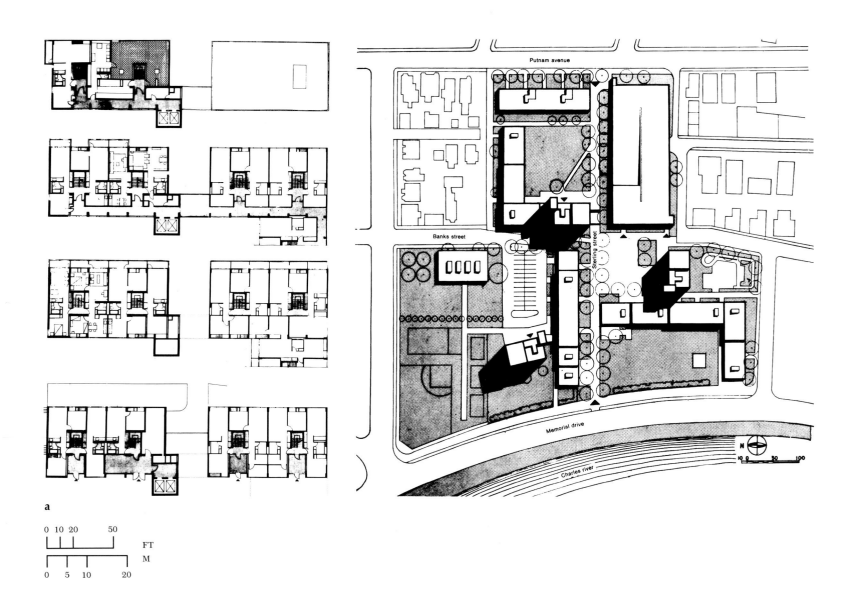

a

0 10 20   50
|__|__|____| FT

                M
|____|____|____|
0   5   10   20

Further Readings

Suntop Homes

Architectural Forum, January 1948, pp. 80–81. [The last of the two special issues of the magazine devoted to Wright.]

Hitchcock, Henry-Russell. *In the Nature of Materials*, p. 98 and ills. 366–368. New York: Duell, Sloan, and Pearce, 1942.

El Pueblo Ribera Court

Gebhard, David. *R. M. Schindler*, p. 69. Los Angeles: Los Angeles County Museum of Art, 1967. [Exhibition catalogue.]

———. *Schindler*, p. 71. New York: Viking, 1972.

"Schindlers Spel Met de Ruimte." *Forum* (Amsterdam), August 1961, pp. 260–263.

Daal en Berg Duplex Houses

Moderne Bouwkunst in Nederland (Rotterdam), 5 (1935), 27–28, 42. [A serial covering modern Dutch building arranged by building type and including photographs and drawings of many of the less well-known buildings of the period.]

Wasmuths Monatshefte für Baukunst und Städtebau (Berlin), 1925, p. 514.

Wasmuths Monatshefte für Baukunst und Städtebau (Berlin), 1927, pp. 114–115.

Group of Court Houses

Blaser, Werner. *Mies van der Rohe*, p. 42. New York: Praeger, 1965.

Kingo Houses

Faber, Tobias. *New Danish Architecture*, pp. 65–67. New York: Praeger, 1968.

Helmer-Petersen, Keld. "A Visit to Denmark: A New Personality, Jørn Utzon," *Zodiac*, 5 (October 1957), 80–85.

Skriver, Poul Erik. "Contemporary Danish Architecture." In *Architects' Year Book 10*, pp. 104–109. London: Elek, 1962.

Weissenhof Exhibition (Mies van der Rohe)

Banham, Reyner. *Theory and Design in the First Machine Age*, pp. 273–278. London: Architectural Press, 1960.

Johnson, Philip C. *Mies van der Rohe*, 2nd ed., pp. 42–48. New York: Museum of Modern Art, 1953.

Teige, Karel. *Nejmensi Byt*, p. 180. Prague, 1932.

Wedepohl, Edgar. "Die Weissenhof-Siedlung der Werkbundausstellung 'Die Wohnung' Stuttgart 1927." *Wasmuths Monatshefte für Baukunst und Städtebau* (Berlin), 1927, pp. 391–402.

Weissenhof Exhibition (J. J. P. Oud)

Hitchcock, Henry-Russell. *J. J. P. Oud*, pp. 28–32. Paris: Editions Cahiers d'Art, 1931.

Wedepohl, Edgar. "Die Weissenhof-Siedlung der Werkbundausstellung 'Die Wohnung' Stuttgart 1927." *Wasmuths Monatshefte für Baukunst und Städtebau* (Berlin), 1927, pp. 391–402.

Vienna Werkbund Exposition (André Lurçat)

"Dreiunddreissig Architekten Bauen in Wien eine Siedlung." *Wasmuths Monatshefte für Baukunst und Städtebau* (Berlin), 1931, p. 460.

Frank, Josef, ed. *Die Internationale Werkbundsiedlung*. Vienna: 1932. [A special publication about the exhibition.]

Ichinomiya

Kenchiku Bunka, June 1961, pp. 89–100.

Tange, Kenzo, and Udo Kultermann. *Kengo Tange: Architecture and Urban Design*, pp. 110–111. New York: Praeger, 1970.

Siedlung Halen

Architectural Design, February 1963, pp. 63–71.

Blumer, J. "Modern Swiss Architecture since 1945." *Architects' Year Book 10*, pp. 143–145. London: Elek, 1962.

Werk, February 1963, pp. 58–71.

Fleet Road Terrace Housing

Architectural Design, September 1967, pp. 423, 432–433.

Rue Franklin Apartments

Banham, Reyner. *Theory and Design in the First Machine Age*, pp. 38–40. London: Architectural Press, 1960.

Champigneulle, Bernard. *Perret*, pp. 16–19. Paris: Arts et Métiers Graphiques, 1959.

Collins, Peter. *Concrete: The Vision of a New Architecture*, pp. 178–184. London: Faber and Faber, 1959.

Avenue de Versailles Apartments

Architectural Review, October 1932, pp. 133–138.

Baumeister, August 1931, p. 327.

Porte Molitor Apartments

Le Corbusier. *Oeuvre complète 1929–1934*, ed. W. Boesiger, pp. 144–153. Zurich: Girsberger, 1935.

Casa Rustici

Koulermos, Panos. "Terragni, Lingeri and Italian Rationalism." *Architectural Design*, March 1963, pp. 120–121.

Zevi, Bruno. *Omaggio a Terragni*, pp. 67–69. Milan: Etas/Kompass, 1968.

Parklaan Apartments

Bromberg, Paul. *Architecture in the Netherlands*, p. 79. The Netherlands Information Bureau, 1944.

Gerretsen, W. J., and J. P. L. Hendriks. *Hedendaagsche Architectuur in Nederland*, p. 144. Amsterdam: Kosmos, 1937.

Moderne Bouwkunst in Nederland (Rotterdam), 4 (1933), pp. 30–31, 52.

Immeuble Villas

Le Corbusier. *Oeuvre complète 1910–1929*, ed. D. Stonorov and W. Boesiger, pp. 40–43. Zurich: Editions d'Architecture, 1929. [See also "Une Ville contemporaine," pp. 34–39; "Immeubles-Villas et Pavillon de l'Esprit Nouveau," pp. 92–99; "Plan Voisin," pp. 114–121.]

Le Corbusier. *The Radiant City*. New York: Orion, 1967.

Spangen Quarter

Fanelli, Giovanni. *Architettura moderna in Olanda*, pp. 43–47. Florence: Marchi and Bertolli, 1968.

Hertzberger, Herman. "Looking for the Beach under the Pavement." *RIBA Journal*, August 1971, p. 330.

Nirwana Apartments

Fanelli, Giovanni. *Architettura moderna in Olanda*, p. 126. Florence: Marchi and Bertolli, 1968.

Jelles, E. J., and C. A. Alberts. "Duiker #1." *Forum* (Amsterdam), November 1971, pp. 38–41. [Special issue.]

Vickery, Robert. "Bijvoet and Duiker." In *Perspecta: The Yale Architectural Journal Volumes 13 and 14*, pp. 151–152. New York: Wittenborn, 1972.

Hansaviertel Apartments

Fleig, Karl. *Alvar Aalto*, pp. 168–173. Zurich: Girsberger, 1963.

Werk, January 1958, pp. 9–12.

Immeuble Clarté

Le Corbusier. *Oeuvre complète 1929–1934*, ed. W. Boesiger, pp. 66–71. Zurich: Girsberger, 1935.

Narkomfin Apartments

Kopp, Anatole. *Ville et revolution*, pp. 150–156. Paris: Editions Athropos, 1967.

Teige, Karel. *Nejmenski Byt*, p. 323. Prague, 1932.

Unité d'Habitation

Besset, Maurice. *Who Was Le Corbusier?* pp. 156–164. Geneva: Skira, 1968.

Le Corbusier. *Oeuvre complète 1938–1946*, ed. W. Boesiger, pp. 172, 193. Zurich: Editions d'Architecture, 1946.

Le Corbusier. *Oeuvre complète 1946–1952*, ed. W. Boesiger, pp. 186–223. Zurich: Girsberger, 1953. [See also pp. 166–171 and "Le Concours de Strasbourg: Unité at Nantes-Renze," pp. 102–111.]

Le Corbusier. *The Radiant City*, p. 43. New York: Orion, 1967.

Harumi Apartment House

Hassenpflug, Gustav, and Paulhans Peters. *Schiebe Punkt und Hügel*, pp. 78–79. Munich: Callwey, 1966.

Kenchiku Bunka, February 1959, pp. 19–38.

Durand Apartments

Le Corbusier. *Oeuvre complète 1929–1934*, ed. W. Boesiger, pp. 160–166. Zurich: Girsberger, 1935.

Le Corbusier. *The Radiant City*, pp. 292–295. New York: Orion, 1967.

Zomerdijkstraat Atelier Apartments

Fanelli, Giovanni. *Architettura moderna in Olanda*, pp. 132–133. Florence: Marchi and Bertolli, 1968.

Moderne Bouwkunst in Nederland (Rotterdam), 5 (1935), 30–32, 42–43.

Hoogbouw Towers

Jelles, E. J., and C. A. Alberts. "Duiker #1." *Forum* (Amsterdam), November 1971, pp. 42–43. [Special issue.] Text in "Duiker #2." *Forum*, January 1972, pp. 138–139.

Vickery, Robert. "Bijvoet and Duiker." In *Perspecta: The Yale Architectural Journal Volumes 13 and 14*, p. 152. New York: Wittenborn, 1972.

Victorieplein Tower

Fanelli, Giovanni. *Architettura moderna in Olanda*, pp. 101–102. Florence: Marchi and Bertolli, 1968.

Moderne Bouwkunst in Nederland (Rotterdam), 4 (1933), pp. 29, 51.

Price Tower

Hitchcock, Henry-Russell. *In the Nature of Materials*, ills. 305–309, 411–413. New York: Duell, Sloan, and Pearce, 1942.

Wright, F. L. *An American Architecture*, ed. Edgar Kaufmann, pp. 114–134. New York: Horizon Press, 1955.

———. *The Story of the Tower*. New York: Horizon Press, 1956.

Neue Vahr Apartments

Bauen und Wohnen, November 1963, pp. 458–460.

Fleig, Karl. *Alvar Aalto*, pp. 262–263. Zurich: Girsberger, 1963.

Hansaviertel Tower

Architetture: Cronache e Storia, December 1961, pp. 528–538.

Bauen und Wohnen, June 1961, pp. 225–228.

Hassenpflug, Gustav, and Paulhans Peters. *Schiebe Punkt und Hugel*, p. 200. Munich: Callway, 1966.

Peabody Terrace

Bastlund, Knud. *José Luis Sert*, pp. 220–231. New York: Praeger, 1967.

Kenchiku Bunka, November 1965, pp. 101–108.

Zodiac, 16 (1966), 24–25.

General Readings

Adler, Leo. *Neuzeitliche Miethauser und Siedlungen*. Berlin: Ernst Pollak, 1931.

Anguissola, L. B. *I 14 anni del piano inacasa*. Rome: Staderini, 1963.

Bachmann, Jul, and Stanislaus von Moos. *New Directions in Swiss Architecture*. New York: Braziller, 1969.

Besset, Maurice. *New French Architecture*. New York: Praeger, 1967.

De Fries, H. *Junge Baukunst in Deutschland*. Berlin: Otto Stollberg, 1926.

Deilmann, Harald, Jörg C. Kirschenmann, and Herbert Pfeiffer. *Wohnungsbau*. Stuttgart: K. Krämer, 1973.

Delvoy, R. L., and M. Culot. *L. H. De Koninck*. Brussels: Architectural Association, Archives of Modern Architecture, 1973.

Fleig, Karl, ed. *Alvar Aalto, 1963–1970*. New York: Praeger, 1971.

Feuerstein, Günther. *New Directions in German Architecture*. New York: Braziller, 1968.

Galardi, Alberto. *New Italian Architecture*. New York: Praeger, 1967.

Hoffmann, Hubert. *Row Houses and Cluster Houses: An International Survey*. New York: Praeger, 1967.

Hoffmann, Ot, and Christoph Repenthin. *Neue urbane Wohnformen*. Gütersloh: Bertelsmann, 1965.

Jensen, Rolf. *High Density Living*. London: Leonard Hill, 1966.

Maxwell, Robert. *New British Architecture*. New York: Praeger, 1972.

Mindlin, Henrique E. *Modern Architecture in Brazil*. New York: Reinhold, 1956.

Moretti, Bruno. *Case d'abitazione in Italia*. Milan: Hoepli, 1939.

Nagel, Siegfried, and Siegfried Linke. *Reihenhäuser, Grouppenhäuser, Hochhäuser*. Gütersloh: Bertelsmann, 1970.

———. *Einfamilienhäuser, Bungalows, Ferienhäuser*. Gütersloh: Bertelsmann, 1968.

Paul, Samuel. *Apartments: Their Design and Development*. New York: Reinhold, 1967.

Pehnt, Wolfgang. *German Architecture, 1960–1970*. New York: Praeger, 1970.

Peter, Peterhans. *Wohnquartiere neue Stadte*. Munich, 1966.

Peters, Paulhans. *Wohnhochhäuser*. Munich: Callwey, 1958.

Roth, Alfred. *La Nouvelle Architecture*. Zurich: Editions d'Architecture, 1948.

Schmitt, K. W. *Multistory Housing*. New York: Praeger, 1966.

Sherwood, Roger. "Modern Housing Prototypes." *Architecture and Urbanism*, March 1975. [Special issue.]

———, ed. *Urban Housing: A Comparative Guide*. Ithaca: Cornell University Department of Architecture, 1970.

Stern, Robert A. *New Directions in American Architecture*. New York: Braziller, 1969.

Sting, Hellmuth. *Grundriss Wohnungsbau*. Stuttgart: Koch, 1975.

Stirling, James. *James Stirling: Buildings and Projects, 1950–1974*. New York: Oxford University Press, 1975.

Suhonen, Pekka. *Utta Suomalaista arkkitehturria*. Helsinki: Kustannusosakeyhtiö Tammi, 1967.

Tempel, Egon. *New Japanese Architecture*. New York: Praeger, 1970.

———. *New Finnish Architecture*. New York: Praeger, 1968.

Van den Broek, J. H. *Habitation*. 3 vols. Amsterdam: Elsevier, 1964.

Woods, Shadrach. *Candilis-Josic-Woods: Building for People*. New York: Praeger, 1968.

Yorke, F. R. S., and Frederick Gibberd. *The Modern Flat*. London: Architectural Press, 1948.

The best periodicals for information on housing are the international architectural serials. Although none are devoted entirely to the subject of housing, most report on a wide range of housing projects and occasionally publish special issues that deal exclusively with some aspect of housing. Examples include the September 1967 issue of *Architectural Design* entitled "Housing Primer," which probably remains the classic reference to low-rise, high-density English housing; the two issues of *Architektur und Wohnform* (February 1969 and February 1970) by Hellmuth Sting, which were perhaps the earliest studies that analyzed housing typologically (these studies were concerned with classification by building and unit types and were later incorporated into Hellmuth's book *Grundriss Wohnungsbau*); and my own study, "Modern Housing Prototypes," in *Architecture and Urbanism* (March 1975).

Most periodicals tend to report more on building in the country in which the periodical is published, although some, such as *Architecture and Urbanism* in Japan, devote considerable space to architecture outside the country of origin. *L'Architecture d'Aujourd'hui* reports on more projects more frequently and covers a greater range of work than any other magazine and is perhaps the best continuing reference to international housing.